**NEW YORK REV
CLASSICS**

IDIOCY

PIERRE GUYOTAT (1940–2020) was born in the village of Bourg-Argental, southwest of Lyon. He started writing and painting in his teens, running away to Paris before he reached the age of majority. In 1960, he was conscripted to fight in the Algerian War; the inhumanity he witnessed there would become one of his central themes as a writer. He was briefly associated with the avant-garde leftism of *Tel Quel* and a member of the Communist Party, but ultimately he pursued his own idiosyncratic course, advocating for human rights and composing books that were dauntless and daring in their ideas and their language alike. He was the author of more than a dozen novels and memoirs, among them *Tomb for 500,000 Soldiers*; *Eden, Eden, Eden*, which was banned in France upon its publication in 1970; and *Coma*, which was awarded the Prix Décembre in 2006. In 2018, he was awarded the Prix Femina spécial for lifetime achievement.

PETER BEHRMAN DE SINÉTY grew up in Maine and lives in Paris, where he teaches at the École Normale Supérieure. His translations include Éric Chevillard's *QWERTY Invectives* and Maël Renouard's *Fragments of an Infinite Memory* (published by New York Review Books).

IDIOCY

PIERRE GUYOTAT

Translated from the French by
PETER BEHRMAN DE SINÉTY

NEW YORK REVIEW BOOKS

New York

THIS IS A NEW YORK REVIEW BOOK
PUBLISHED BY THE NEW YORK REVIEW OF BOOKS
207 East 32nd Street, New York, NY 10016
www.nyrb.com

The first sketches of this book were read by Donatien Grau to our friend Azzedine Alaïa, at work in his atelier. —Pierre Guyotat

Peter Behrman de Sinéty wishes to thank Helen Plotkin for accompanying him throughout this translation.

Copyright © 2018 by Éditions Grasset et Fasquelle
Translation copyright © 2025 by Peter Behrman de Sinéty
All rights reserved.

Originally published in the French language as *Idiotie*.

Library of Congress Cataloging in Publication Control Number: 2025006862

ISBN 978-1-68137-919-7
Available as an electronic book; ISBN 978-1-68137-920-3

The authorized representative in the EU for product safety and compliance is eucomply OÜ, Pärnu mnt 139b-14, 11317 Tallinn, Estonia, hello@eucompliancepartner.com, +33 757690241.

Printed in the United States of America on acid-free paper.
10 9 8 7 6 5 4 3 2 1

CONTENTS

The Lice Girl · 1

Laideronette · 9

Sophie · 21

The Casket · 26

Rue du Jour · 39

Prisons · 57

Worksites · 66

Algiers · 74

The "Sphynx" · 80

Interrogation · 83

Solitary Confinement · 100

Independence · 109

Exodus · 123

The Lice Girl

PARIS, AUTUMN 1958, under the Pont de l'Alma, around midnight, third night outdoors in our escape to Paris from Lyon, where, after nine years of boarding school, I am now a student in my final year of lycée, living with my father's younger brother, a psychiatrist.

On our tent floor that covers the cobblestones between two flows of dried piss—fling yourself into filth, approach it, touch it, handle it; to live at last as a man comes only through this contact, this partaking of misery; the saints sanctified themselves by it, and therefore so should I, but how? confront my taste for clarity and order with it—we slip into our sleeping bags. François falls asleep; in the pocket of my jacket rolled up in my backpack I have a small black-and-white photo of his fifteen-year-old sister stepping toward me as I snap a close-up of her laughing little face, blond in real life. Boat lights shine against the black undersides of the arches; the water slaps at stone—drowned corpses, carcasses of beaten dogs; farther on, the lights of houseboats and barges mingle with the beams of the Champ de Mars spotlights on the tower.

He sleeps, head outside the bag atop the hood, mouth open; I hear his belly grumble: since noon, nothing but a baguette for two big eaters. Tomorrow, hunger.

If I merely doze off then death is the one that grabs me, drags me to her abyss beyond the world; go to sleep quickly and soundly where she can't reach me. Silently, so she can't find me.

The sounds of the capital recede; farther on, beyond Passy, lives one of my mother's sisters; in the southern suburb of Bagneux, one of her brothers, my godfather, a hero of the French Resistance; across the Seine, in Saint-Germain, lives one of my father's sisters, a member of the same Resistance cell, Ravensbrück survivor, not far from the street where the Gestapo arrested my mother's youngest brother, later deported and killed at Oranienburg-Sachsenhausen; farther on, in Boulogne, another of my mother's brothers, wounded in the Forest of Halatte in May 1940, Free French Forces, Leclerc's division, the Fezzan, wounded in the Vosges in autumn 1944, service in Indochina, Algeria...

And yet, though I love and admire them, I've already stopped wanting to see them, and at the instant when, with my mother dead, my escape will become an inner imperative, I'll face this still so distant capital next year alone and without their help.

Each winter, journeying from our low mountain town—the setting of Barbey d'Aurevilly's *Story Without a Name*, where my mother, born near Warsaw herself, gave birth to the six of us and assisted our father in his work as a doctor—she would come to Paris to see her sisters. One of them, having taken the veil on the day of the Munich "Agreement," is a cloistered nun at the Benedictine abbey in Jouarre, in Seine-et-Marne.

From one of these visits, in 1954, at a time when, partially abandoning gouache and drawing, I was writing poetry every day, she brought me the numbered Mercure de France edition of the works of Arthur Rimbaud as a belated fourteenth-birthday present.

Two months since she died, my youngest brother not yet eleven years old, and I eighteen. Afflicted for seven years, bedridden in March, she was nursed by our two eldest sisters. Our eldest brother had already served nearly thirty months as a soldier in Algeria, and my mother, a historian at heart, lamented the lack of order, the fragility of political power at the end of the French Fourth Republic, then rejoiced at the firstlings of Charles de Gaulle's return.

One morning, back from a bicycle camp in Touraine, I came down at her call from the attic room I shared with my dear youngest brother at the top of our apartment in the center of town, and found her suffering from pleurisy, lying in bed. She wanted us to talk, her and me, about one of my holiday writing assignments: "Is Imagination a Creative Force?" Did she want to reassure herself of my determination to devote my life to creating? Before dying, did she—who understood the world only through the sacred, through its holy servants, celebrants of faith, charity, courage, and beauty, its artists, heroes, saints illustrious and modest, and who therefore felt all the more horror, revulsion, and disgust at everything that harms the sacred: death camps, extermination camps—did she want to show me, who knew her pain but did not foresee it would end in death, her fear but also her pride upon seeing me set out to stake my life, my fate, our family honor, on inspiration alone?

Before I knocked at the door to their room, filled with light in all seasons and overlooking the church against a dark mountain, I knew she was powdering her face, already slightly emaciated, in her mirror that she already struggled to hold in her own fingers, and arranging her hair that her sisters and brothers also have, dark, rich, dazzling. I entered. From the steeple that rings the quarter hours night and day, a peal of bells for a baptism shook the windows behind the gauze curtains; on the mantelpiece facing the bed were objects from Poland, from Russia; on the wall above them, a gilded metal Virgin in a black mahogany display case; on the bedside table, among other books, *Olympio: The Life of Victor Hugo* by André Maurois, which she and my father had bought in order to read up on what to do with a child poet; to the right of the bed, a diamond-point armoire which, like the Empire secretary in the living room, is forbidden to us, and which holds a casket of receipts and ready cash in an inner drawer.

I sat beside the bed, the pages of my essay in hand; a little of her shoulders and breast was bare; I had never seen her in bed except when, on New Year's morning, we would come to kiss her and my father, and when, in late May 1942, she gave birth to my brother and held him close to her, shoulders and breast already half-bare before us like the Nativity scene, and I, two and a half years old, in tears, reached out my arms to her but she kept her own close to her newborn...

The revolving beam of a belated tourist boat's red lantern whips over us, François keeps his mouth open, a patch of light upon his radiant teeth, I shut my eyes, open them: a shape has slipped behind my head from the base of the arch; I flip round in the bag, prop myself up, elbows against the cobblestones. From a pile of rags, a plump hand, its bare arm marked with scars, lifts the tatters to the sniffer; I follow the hand to the large turned-up nostrils where a filthy-nailed finger digs; above, curly locks, slightly greasy, poke from under the raised earflaps of an army surplus hat; lashes long as fakes beat against cheekbones whose pink appears in the red patch of light; the finger picks at the lashes: lice?

During the Occupation and right after the war, because of shortages and rationing, scabies infested more bodies than in peacetime: many of us, in primary school, scratched at our bodies, large heads thin legs, weak with rickets; Marie-Rose Mite and Lice Powder wafted through classrooms and schoolyards.

… The body moves, all at once, goes down beneath the once more scattered rags, beneath the stench of dried piss I smell another of perfume, of filth, and of something unknown to me: Could it be the smell of those discharges that a few of us, upon returning to boarding school on Sunday evenings, try to describe as issuing from the intimate parts, the secret places, of the girls they brag of having seen "topped" by young workers at dances in villages and city outskirts? The smell which, three years ago, returning from England, in the hold of the ferry, I caught wind of from the tampon of the sleeping girl?

The lice leap on the nostril hairs, on the fine fuzz between the nose and the curl of the large, fresh lips trembling from a nightmare in which you have to speak, find the words that save you in the face of the monster. Lower, the buttocks arch in a long purr, under the tatters I see a pair of short shorts clinging to it, worn into holes from back to front, their creases reddened by the patch of light from the boat which comes to a stop; in the splay of the thighs, a button dangles from the fly; the seam between fly and leg-hem is torn; hairs poke from it; toward the slope of the thighs, a scrap of fabric hugs a bristly fold; a gesture brings the knee flush to the stomach; I see through holes the bottom edge of the buttocks, the line of the crotch, clogged with dirt, crusted, toward the organ where the fleece glistens, damp, greasy, in the red halo of the boat which starts off again in a plume of smoke; the vermin have the run of the rags; above, the body moves again, an arm rises back out of the pile, above the chest and head, the hand clutches at the cobblestones; from the remains of a white blouse under a tattered red jacket, one tawny-ringed white breast appears and settles itself in the gaps between the cobblestones, the other at liberty; an eyelid rises, the eye gazes at the cobblestones then at my gaze; large, blue; the arm shields the eye, the wrist criss-crossed with cuts... below, I adjust my glasses, there again, the vermin leap, but nothing like the lice or fleas whose revels on the napes of my deskmates I used to watch as a child, right after the Occupation: What are these vermin that seem to suit this girl so well she purrs?

We wake to the clamor, car horns, bike horns, bells, tinkles, shouts, whistles; empty pockets, identity card and photos alone in a flat wallet, where and what to eat? We wash at a fountain in the Tuileries Garden where paupers delouse and bathe their dogs. We walk, guts in a knot, toward the Place Clichy; the curtains of carnival stalls draw open: fake monsters, strippers so close we can almost hear their flesh—young, not so young, sour—shivering in the drafts of still cold air. Hearing us speak of our hunger, a man leads us through curtains to a space where, placing a microphone in front of our mouths, he records our voices in counterpoint repeating what he heard us say; a small payment—which could become a large one if we follow him up a street that rises toward a gilt-framed door: our two hearts, François's slow, mine erratic, beat as one for once. François shakes his index finger from side to side. The man takes back the coins he flashed at us in his open palm. But why does he offer, to me alone—do I really have the face of a poet, when I wish I had a whore's—that I write him a few come-hither slogans for his girls in exchange for some crisp bills whose smell teases my nostrils? But, in solidarity with François, disappointed not to have been chosen, I decline.

Eat on the run, change districts; go back toward Les Halles; scraps, vegetables, meat, everywhere on the stalls, the freshest on top, iffiest on bottom; around the kiosks and ice-cream carts, broken cones—we pick some up, scrunch them between our teeth; hunger, of a day or two, heightens the senses, the will. A big ruddy man in a leather apron has us tidy away some cases in his bar-restaurant's back courtyard, then, turning to me, he has me write up his menus "with a touch of fancy," but before eating, as if he knew how hunger whets the imagination that a full belly puts to sleep. Two plates of shepherd's pie, then, at sight of our eagerness, a third to split between us. Above the bar, the radio rebroadcasts an excerpt from the press conference in which Charles de Gaulle offers the Algerian rebels the "peace of the brave."

We have to return to Lyon for the resumption of classes at the lycée, with no ticket, with no money; at the Porte d'Italie we put out our thumbs; a truck picks us up and drops us off in Burgundy at dusk, on the banks of a canal, at the place of some acquaintances of our driver's, who sets out again to deliver his cargo of meat from the north to the Swiss canton of Jura. A little house, a large canal lock, out-of-breath children back from fishing; a truck is to stop by tomorrow at dawn, and arrive in Lyon by late morning.

Between two operations of the lock an early dinner, beef stew, local wine, children past their bedtime pattering above us. The young husband—exempt from long military service as sole provider for his own family and for his sisters and brothers, one of whom was drafted at the age of eighteen to serve in Algeria—a port-wine stain on his sturdy neck near the shoulder, goes out into the night and comes back with a snake, green-scaled, yellow-bellied, in his open hands. The baby at the breast of the very young mother flinches, but she, with a smile on her small rosy mouth, presses her breast for more milk. And, with a voice that goes with the sound of the water outside, she tells us—looking into her husband's eyes and upon all the rest of his body—that in addition to his position as a lockkeeper, he catches snakes for the Institut Pasteur in Paris, and that we will be sleeping tonight above his stockroom; the snake coils itself around an arm, the husband raises it toward her neck, the creature curls itself there, its head beneath her well-formed ear where I hear the husband's breath and words, love spirit, beside her on the pillow; the husband takes little ones out of his peacoat pocket, snakelets still unsteady, but they know how to curl around his wrists; female snake, or male? Not enough venom in the fangs at the back of the little ones' jaws: pet creatures, to habituate the children and close acquaintances. After filth in Paris, contact with the reptile. First, touch the body of the animal; the husband holding the head, I grasp it too low, near the tail, the snake flinches, the jaws open out of the husband's fist, and he says, in a wine-breath—even without an *r* in the sentence, I recognize the accent of my grandfather, born in Autun, Rue aux Rats: "You touched its genitals, it's a female and you caused it pain."

The little wife—so close to us in age but so distant in condition: "Don't worry him, you're exaggerating, he didn't hurt it that much!"

The snakelets grow restless; the husband, snake on his neck, has them drink from a bowl of milk that the wife, cradling her baby in her arms, has gone to fetch in the kitchen, where the half-open window overlooks the canal.

Snakelets back in his pocket—she holds her baby and lights the way for us from the threshold with a big army flashlight—he leads us into a shed beneath a tall beech tree that quivers in the rising wind. Below, on the ground floor, set on trestles in the dirt, are the tight-grated cages where the vipers knot and unknot themselves, venom fortified through confinement; a ladder leads to the upper story with its floor covered in summer straw; we open and spread out our sleeping bags; the husband, snakes and snakelets back in their cages, shuts the door on us. Through a hole in the cob wall, we see the lights of the house switch off, then all the other lights of the lock; the wind takes hold, we hear the branches shake outside and, between the gusts, beneath the layer of straw exhaling a remnant of summer heat, the crawling of the snakes in their cages, males to females.

Sheltered from the wind, at peace in the smell of the nourishing wheat—trysting-place of guilty love, blood on gold, house of refuge for the hunted—our bellies full, we fall asleep quick. In my dream appears the viper that, as a little child, at the end of one of the Bible readings my mother would hold for us, I named "Athalia," after the queen of Judah, forsaker of the one true God, follower of Baal, the enemy's idol whose very name sounds demonic, child-swallower, forger of lies. In summer, the viper would hang down from a hole at the back of the garden wall, all day long, glinting dark red, sometimes raising a third of its body and holding itself rigid, head shimmering and tongue vibrating, in a horizontal to-and-fro: for in the flowerbeds, though distant, a little rodent or sparrow quivered, fascinated, heart fluttering, by that which would pierce it with its fangs and deliver it from a life of being coveted for its flesh. A gust of wind rustles the roof tiles; in the lull, I hear raised voices, male and female intertwined; I fall back asleep, the sunrise will quiet the wind.

On waking, we help the husband load the cages into his van.

At breakfast, the café au lait steams; the baby feeds; in the silence of the husband and wife, I hear the sound of sucking. Her tired face moves forward and back, lids lowered, above her dazzling breast; his voice holds the trace of a trembling; the baby's eye, its mouth detached from the nipple, already looks from one gaze to the other; barge horns blast on the canal; nothing is surer than the laying in of supplies, a baby, a nation.

The tractor-trailer brakes on the incline: she, the baby back in its cradle, white blouse, red pants, touches the straps of our backpacks, breathes a faint mist from her painted lips. As her so fair body comes close to mine, full-grown, my muscles loosen at this scented heat like when, already long ago now, I would come close to my mother to read the same page with her and could hear her brain, little by little, thinking each phrase. But here, it's her forward breasts, their contour, the trace of the nipple, milk on the light fabric and a heat issuing from farther below, her trembling in the gathering light as she breathes into her palms. So near this nourishing flesh which it would be possible to embrace, penetrate at any moment, how can I create what I want: a glance from her would release all creative tension, penetrate my inner vision and, by this violation, sap all its secret strength; and there would be pleasure in the place of desire.

Laideronette

IN THE heat of mid-July 1959, the carton, released from the bungee cords and jostling in my arms, exhales a scent of drapery laced with the scent of the thighs of Laideronette, who packed and tied it.

The Rue Marie-Rose is empty. Passing through one of the neighboring streets, I heard, from an open sixth floor, between plants suspended from the shutters, the arpeggios of Robert Schumann's Mignon, from his *Album for the Young*—a piece I learned with my mother on our Pleyel piano, and which I imagine Schumann to have composed with one of his many children sitting on his knees and tapping out the high note of each arpeggio to form the melody...

Seventh floor, no elevator. Up there, beneath the stairhead skylights, a door is open, a sewing machine purrs, a little girl in braids bustles about, puts some packages away on the tiled floor; I set down the carton of buttons, galloons, embroideries; from the back of the garret, a weary voice, as if derailed, says: "Give the young man a glass of peppermint..."; the little girl touches and appraises the lapels of my blazer between two already needle-pricked fingers, the last piece of clothing my mother picked out for me, which I keep on despite the heat, during my delivery errands on my Solex; a big yellow-and-white cat mews among the pairs of slippers. "She's been scared since the planes flew by... there's no one left in the building, they're all at the parade"; the glass of peppermint finished, the little girl hugged so tightly in my arms she turns pale, I go back outside. By the sidewalk, on the ground floor, facing the Solex, is a window where a sudden gust of wind or an aftershock of the rumble of the jet planes has jarred open the shutters; an odor of suntan lotion wafts from the sooty opening; I look in and listen: a foot, naked, pale, hangs from a red shape above a fringed rug; the sound of a record turning with no music in the half-light. My gaze forces its way into the darkness, like entering a church, then rises, front-angle, along the toes, the heel marked with dust, the foot, the ankle, the long calf, the unfolded knee with its prominent kneecap, the pimply thigh, the naked fleece, black shading into blue, bright, curly above the organ in bold outline; a finger is caught there and spreads the red lappets; the belly, flat, breathes between a pair of thin hips; the snail-shaped belly button; beyond, the small, hard breasts tremble at the irregular breathing which causes the nipples to shine—by what light, from the back of the room or from a corner?—as the two ringed fingers of the other hand ease off from fondling them; white-gray throat, bare neck like a tube, round chin, very well-defined lips, the remainder of a lit cigarette at the lower lip, cheeks batted by big fake lashes; the body, slender, shudders from a dream, or from a flea; curls of lustrous hair, blue-black with lathery glints, set off a smooth brow, radiant, large, domed; everything inside it seems in order there: will, desire, past, future, even the dreams; a dream or a draft of wind arrives—blown from the back of the room whose depth I can't determine, but with an aftersmell of public excrement and creolin well known to me from boarding school, and soon from army service, and which is the sign not of a private bathroom but of a communal back-courtyard toilet —and this causes the body to swing to its right, the round buttocks illuminate the red shape as a coverlet slipping from the bed, a pink sheet-fold, the striped-blue pillow, a chair and a pair of underwear, very short, pink, with no lace, hanging, top right, from the back of the chair. I look for the bra, but on the back of the same chair, top left, hangs another pair of underwear, white, just as short but bordered with lace, fluttering a little; in the half-light a shadow moves along the back wall; a naked body, very pale, appears; out of a tuft of hair the same dark color as the one on the bed, a member stands erect until a rough hand tucks it back; the body bends, a hand raises the pickup arm of the record player which I can't see; the record stops, along with the sound of the empty turning; the hips are long, the buttocks hollowed, the face turns toward the half-open shutters: same mouth, same nostrils, same brow, same curls of hair, but no fake lashes on the large, forthright eyes, wrathful, pitch-black pupils, white pink blue, and the brow furrowed; the shoulders are a little larger, downy hair lies above the spill of the upper lip, around the flat nipples, the belly button, and thick in the groin; at the smell of wiped excrement, the body on the sheet stirs, a leg stretches itself from the full thigh, the foot explores the edge of the faded red coverlet, a yawn concludes in a little belch; the standing body stretches itself, arms outspread, hands clasped above the head, hairy armpits, bent knees—the body pounces on the mattress, on the girl, the twin, the two bodies coil into each other, the legs, his hairy, hers smooth, intertwine, rub together, I hear the mouths kiss, the saliva slap at flesh, the teeth tinkle, the hands grasp, clutch, caress, claw, lash, the hairs rub against each other, the joints tighten, loosen, knock together, the skin rolls back, slides, the long hips rise, the narrow buttocks drop, rise again, drop again, the downy hair at the curve of the back shines with sweat, the girl-leg falls back, soft on the edge that's red, I hear whimpers, choked panting, moans, muffled laughter, open laughter—which one of them softly farts?

I shut my nostrils at the thrust of the groin and its aftershocks, I'll breathe again once the two bodies fall side by side: to step back from the opening would alter the light that bathes them and make him turn his head to the street. Would I have time to grab my Solex and start off toward the intersection?

But she, shoving his chest away with her clenched fist, sinks deep into the mattress: Is she forcing him to pull out his glutted member? Him—I can see him more clearly; his loins buck; his mouth opens again—he lets out a little guttural cry; the only thing I can see between their tufts of hair is their two fists knocking together, a flash of red;

it's that he wants to take her again; she, with a thrust of her hips, sits up, rolls to her side onto the coverlet that spills over a scrap of yellow linoleum nailed to the musty wood floor, crouches, crawls on all fours toward the back; her high buttocks disappear in the shadowy light; I do my best not to already see the open hole her excrement will come out of; but now her face turns back, above a breast tucked under her arm that reaches to the floor, eyes wide open, pupil and cornea shining, she glares toward the light that filters through the shutters—has she seen me, and why is she wiggling her ass, with a speck of froth shining at the right edge of her mouth? What can she see of me in the gap between the shutters? Hair, brow, eyes, glasses, nostrils, mouth, chin, bare neck... my lower body hidden by the wall.

Him—sitting on the sheet, forearm against his raised knees, his member stiff against the folds below his navel, misty eyes behind the smoke from the cigarette he holds in his large trembling hand—with a giant adolescent cracking his voice fills the room: "It'll all still be here for you when you get back, puss."

What savage children await to be born of this incest between two defecations in a back-courtyard shitter!

Long lashes lowered, he begins to bite at his kneecaps.

I step back, grab the Solex, ride over to the Avenue Bosquet where I have to help an old dowager write a detective novel. I climb the two flights of stairs carpeted in red velvet; the maid answers the door, a little blond woman whose breasts are fragrant with her cooking—of which I would gladly eat, along with the dainty fingers that made it. She leads me in her white apron to the back of the large apartment lined with paintings of ancestors from merely the nineteenth century; in a bow window with red, yellow, green stained-glass panes, the old woman sits with a black ribbon tied around her neck, a paintbrush in her raised hand before a heavy easel; I step around a black mahogany table covered in green felt on which rests a big typewriter—which would be of more use to me than to her, but I can't afford to buy even a secondhand one; in a cylindrical cage the top of which is

LAIDERONETTE · 13

in darkness, a green parrot with red cheeks holds forth from its repertoire of moderate sounds gleaned from the hushed apartment: the old woman's cough, the creaking floors, the hubbub of voices on the avenue, the paintbrush twirling in its pot, my footsteps; a brief flashback of the twins' embrace makes me shudder in the heat, more intense here: I haven't retied my tie; I step toward the old woman, who, without letting go of her paintbrush, offers me her other hand which I kiss as I have done since I was a child tall enough to do so: the canvas smells good but the work is ugly, the coat of paint thick, the motif so secret that nothing of it can be discerned; the parrot panics, beats its wings, bites here and there; I sit down at the table; the sheet with the recently interrupted text lies on the roller; I want to take a new sheet and type out some of the text I've been working on in my head during my errands and keep the paper for myself: but it's already time to resume this affair of hers in which she wants everything to take place on Rue Montorgueil, where she passed one night during the interwar years in a taxi taking her home from a Boulevards theater with her husband, also a rentier. And she wants it all to take place in the milieu of the oystermen, because a protest brought their taxi to a standstill at Au Rocher de Cancale; we have arrived at a rough sketch of a love intrigue between an oysterman and his young half-niece from Brittany: the old woman, paintbrush in hand, head doddling from one part of the painting to another, proposes a sentence and then ideas for a paragraph; I propose variants; accepted; I type them; from the old woman's broken voice emerges a new phrase, crucial, which delights her, and of which the last words are "at the heart of love"; the parrot repeats them, my fingers, sweating at the keys, type them, but in my ear I hear "the hurt of love, the hurt of love," along with the sound of the excrement blasting from the buttocks of the twin sister over there on Rue Marie-Rose, and my lips mouth each word in turn. The session finished, the hand re-kissed, I return to the entrance, in the cool of the air: the little maid—what can she possibly be preparing for a single old lady only concerned with herself—is waiting for me there, payment envelope in hand, unsealed; I don't take it; she, her rosy cheek blushing, raises it to her mouth, licks the edges, licks again, presses the two edges down; the glue will blot out the saliva...which the heat will have dried away; the alcove where she sleeps in the entrance is open, some undergarments lie on a slip of open sheets, a sound of water rises deep in the half-light.

I return to Rue Marie-Rose; the shutters are closed over the closed window; I enter the back courtyard: empty shitter, shut.

I meet up with some friends, couriers, students, near Vincennes; motorcycles, my Solex; Laideronette rides double with Liba, shorts to shorts, on a 125cc motorcycle. In the two months since I ran away from Lyon to live in Paris, I've been a courier for a little couture house on Boulevard Montparnasse owned by a foppishly elegant man who, on the first day, sent me—hungry, with no advance or tip—to buy him sandwiches that he ate bent over his patterns and samples; but that evening when he learned I had no place to sleep, he made a spot for me at the back of the shop where I slept fitfully on a pile of linens, tormented by the image of my father sleeping alone in the bedroom next to their own, the "free bedroom" that belonged to my eldest brother—now a soldier in western Algeria—my father's anguish interwoven with my own.

In seven days of errands—delivering from wholesalers and semi-wholesalers to attic seamstresses in the city and city outskirts, from deluxe hotels to luxury stores, from the center to the suburbs, blackened Paris, black-green Paris, factories, chimney stacks, lines of smoke—I came to understand the capital and its environs. At each place, a small tip, a glass of lemonade or peppermint; in a tiny old shop of umbrellas, galloons, and haberdashery near Saint-Roch, I lingered at the counter; large tip in my pocket, glass of peppermint finished; on the walls, framed photos with sepia colonial scenes. The owner—round eyeglasses, gray smock, beret, born in the Limoges, three cousins burned alive as small children in Oradour—drew aside two curtains hung on golden rings; he began to speak, his hand trembling on his glass. His wife, born of a Vietnamese family that fled to France, stood in a black polka-dotted dress, a red carnation in her black chignon, and turned her hand to and fro upon the shoulder of their daughter, all fleshy, a patch of downy hair verging on whiskers above her upper lip, very dark hairs poking from under the slanted armpit, nicely raised breasts beneath the gray undershirt, pelvis arched on the chair, in short red shorts with the hem tucked up to the slope of the thigh; she looked up at me from her sewing machine, specks of blue shining in her fawn-colored eyes between her slanted lids, two furrows down her brow; my blazer and manners put her at ease; later, in the breeze of a metro grate, I settled her on my luggage rack, bare-legged; we crossed the Seine. At the Comptoir de la Croix Rouge where a few other couriers and I sometimes swap errands, Liba, a Pole extracted from Poland by priests, lured her with his beautiful broad speech and the promise of his red lips...

We head for the banks of the Marne beyond Lagny, dinner in our backpacks; the 125cc motorcycle leads the way or follows behind; Laideronette, so named for her hairiness and her little snout in honor of Ravel's *Mother Goose* suite, rests her head, eyes shut, in the crook of the shoulder of Liba the Beautiful, whose pelvis we will see, late in the night, come glistening from the shadows of Saint-Germain-des-Prés, cigarette smoke above his ringleted head. Swarms of insects wheel beneath the branches of our swimming spot: beyond the tunnel under the Metz–Paris line, the little cliff-bank filled with ratholes slopes toward the river whose midstream current has been our haunt since the end of spring; farther on, an abandoned hotel, in ruins, shrubs growing against the remains of wallpapered walls, debris of porcelain jugs, tarnished copper pots hanging from a piece of wall, a wooden staircase spiraling toward the caved-in roof, frames without paintings or photographs, excrement on the hearth, snakes' slough on the bedding. Laideronette undresses there, with little cries; in a two-piece suit, not so much naked as short-skirted, she swims, huffs between us: me and someone, me and Liba. In the midstream current toward the west, speedboats race along, bows aloft; the waves splash some adolescents near the shore; a few of them are "Arab-skinned," a skin that, at the time, arouses fear.

Before us, muskrats float, paw like mad, whiskery muzzles above the water; Liba mimics them; they turn and paddle toward us; Laideronette loses her breath; we have to swim back to the riverbank, carry her panting up between the ratholes to the grass: a fold of the swell of her organ quivers outside the hemline beneath the hairs wet with mud; I put my fingers there to pull the hem back over it, Liba's hand lays itself on mine, forces my fingers to enter under the soaked cloth, my index finger touching the approach to the sensitive slit beneath the thick hair... I feel myself go pale as the color returns to Laideronette's cheeks; her entire body trembles; Liba's fingers unlace themselves from mine; all wet, Laideronette still smells of haberdashery, lightly of fur; her round breasts quiver beneath her blue suit-top, one of them in the golden pre-sunset light of summer, the other in my shadow; should I lay my palm there as upon the lit and unlit portions of the globe—Limousin and Vietnam? The muskrats turn in the current; does she feel my fingers on the drenched fur of her organ? As he crouches beside me, his broad chest still dripping with water, Liba's breath passes between my ears, a remnant of his effort while swimming, but also, deeper, nearer, the trace of a twofold desire: Does he want—not only for me to take the girl, but also—to lure me into letting myself be handled and taken during those nights of his from which he returns to us with furious eyes, crease furrowed from the right corner of his mouth to his thick nostril, when we meet up again in the mornings, wheel to wheel? The others have scattered into the hotel grove; a train from the east rushes along, whistles beyond the corn, then above the little tunnel; I don't dare withdraw my fingers; we might feel the sliding, she and I, like a ploy for pleasure, and on a body faint with weakness, young, of mixed blood, colonial... respect is stronger than desire; the clatter of the end of the train brings all three of us back to our feet.

Past midnight, we leave Liba to primp his crotch on Saint-Germain-des-Prés—but, back then, what do I know about that? I, who have daydreamed since puberty of brothels overflowing with the seed of melancholy captive adolescents, of the adult patrons who delight in it, and of the male-on-male couplings their seed excites and lubricates? Nothing, as of yet, and nothing for a long time still: at most, a few sacrilegious words, whose mere utterance to myself annuls their organic reality.

Riding along the Right Bank of the floodlit Seine, among the last groups of stragglers from the Bastille Day balls, I can sense that my father, back from his last house calls in the mountains alight beneath the full moon, is climbing at this hour into his sleigh bed, in a white nightshirt, alone, tormented because I have run away; I can feel his effort to climb in, to lie down there; I feel his muscles relax, his memory summon up facts of their love that I can only imagine, facts of the war, of the conception of each of us, of our fetal growth within the womb of his *Darling*—in rare moments of weakness, far away from him, I sometimes call my mother, his wife, by that name—the fact of our births, of our first words, our first steps; I feel his mouth frame fragments of prayer or rejection until he falls asleep with the terror of his body turning onto its side and finding no touch of her hip there, not even her imprint on the sheets when she's risen to stand dreaming at the window... but how could he concern himself with such a big, ungainly adolescent as me, born of his seed and doing it no honor, stammering out rhythms, murmuring melodies, a virgin, incapable—from boredom or because there's always something better to do—of enduring more than seven minutes in philosophy or mathematics—incapable of diving from more than waist-high, of mounting a girl... me, his son? Him, a man of knowledge, a lover, fiancé, husband, son-in-law, generous brother-in-law, frisked, hands up against the wall, with other men of the neighborhood in front of the Milice Française and the Gestapo—us, little children, crossing the square on our way to safe haven—servant of the commune, the district, the department, servant of the poor, midwife of generations, master setter of fractures incurred through real work, seven years of anguish at the side of our afflicted mother, protector of his father, of his mother...

Two days after I ran away, warned that my father and an uncle from Paris were looking for me, and afraid they might spot me in the metro or on a bus or out on the streets, with Paris having become menacing, I took a taxi for the first time in my life to escape to the outskirts. At a stoplight on Carrefour Médicis, I saw them pass before me on the crosswalk, my father falter there, straighten himself up again, his hand on a post. I held myself back from getting out and running to his side; back in Paris a few days later, during one of my errands, I parked beside that same post, laid my palm there: if there is a God who sees my acts, let him judge my heart!

Past the Pont de l'Alma, I ride up toward my place in Passy, a garret room on Rue Chernoviz: water tap on the downstairs landing; no table, I write sitting on my bed, against my knees; a skylight the size of a book. As I enter the street, I see at the far end a man in a three-piece suit consulting a notebook in front of the courtyard doorway, in the heat. The police? Yesterday, still a year and a half away from legal adulthood, I sent my father a petition for emancipation, with a general delivery address in the Bourse district, where some friends have agreed to reconnoiter the area before I present my card there. Turn back or continue on? The cars along both sidewalks look empty. I turn back, ride toward Trocadéro, circle around with the other vehicles until I calm my pounding heart, come back to the street. The man is there, sitting on the hood of a sedan, smoking a cigar whose smell reaches me at the Carrefour Passy. I advance toward my door, but still on the Solex. He shakes out his match, advances toward me, holds out his hand: "Pierre?" It's the detective my father set on my trail with the help of one of my uncles two months ago. Young, having found me, assured of a handsome fee, he wants to have a good time; his car, a secondhand convertible, is parked on Rue Passy; blasts of hot air scuttle up from the Seine. A girl, this time fully Asian—pale breasts in a black silk blouse, thighs hugged by something yet unseen in small towns, blue jeans, a gray-pink mouth opening against a lock of black hair freed from its bun, and, higher, eyelids, slit so narrow that only the black center of the iris shows—sits on the buff leather seat: Does he want to use her to lure me someplace where my father will appear in all his wrath? I bring the Solex back to my doorway, set it on its kickstand; with the still damp bathing suit in my blazer pocket, I walk back to the convertible. The girl makes a place for me between him and her: leather, light tweed, cigar, her hair, her skin so sparsely covered or tightly pressed on sweat, the mahogany dashboard—everything smells of urban vice; I squeeze my shoulders together, my elbows, my hands; we drive through the asphalt breeze toward the Place de l'Étoile; he comes to a stop, parks the convertible on a street that slopes toward the Champs-Élysées; she gets out, takes my hand in hers, small, tender; her nail, which I see is rosy-pink and long, slides along a line of my hand: the doorman, adolescent, gallooned with gold, pockmarks on his fresh face, raises a corner of the red curtain for us; I want to run away; the stairs drop steeply down, gold and red; slow music rises from a dark pit pierced by flickers of light; girls, women, shoulders bared to the edge of their breasts, wreaths of smoke, sobs of a saxophone; the girl starts down the stairs, takes my hand again, tugs me.

Until now, I've only lingered around dance halls on the banks of the Saône upriver from Lyon and Marne above the confluence with the Seine, stepped inside, kept to the edges of the dance floors, watched the ebb and flow of the couples there, he never the same, she never the same, free, all of them manual laborers, apprentices, of easy flesh—the crates I've handled at the wharf market in Lyon, the Solex and cartons I handle in Paris, haven't sufficed to wear in my own flesh, too steeped in art, too stiff with constraints of "class," too shaped by ancestors from within. Reading, seeing, and hearing human and divine passions exaggerated and transfigured, novels, tragedies, paintings, sculptures, operas, oratorios, has embarrassed my limbs, weighed down my spontaneous will; my experience of fulfilled pleasure, solitary but peopled with written figures, and its inevitable depressive aftereffects, its punishment, a repugnance for all texts—along with the tedium of wasting time that might be allotted to the mind—has kept me on the periphery of the embrace: And how could I play an honorable role there, without an ardor equal to the raptures of the heroes of love? And, well schooled in the practice of getting a stiff and lasting hard-on for the creatures of my imagination for as long as I can make them speak and, therefore, make myself write to give them pleasure—and dignity though art—would I have as much strength, as much endurance, in real life, with what others call living things? At this time in my life, I still know too little about the things of the world, about humans, consciousness, nature, the antipodes; and the imagination makes up for this deficiency, the act itself of imagining, not its creatures; and, above all, though I know how to have patience—hope, not patience—I believe solely in inspiration, solely in what is done in a single act, without interruption: How can one decompose an act, if logic is a flash of light, a dazzlement, a dance, a laugh, an attunement with God the Creator...?

To introduce an instruction manual, when all is electric, shorts the circuit; to capitulate to real life—the couple calmly composing its compromises—is sorrow and tearing asunder for a child of God, who Speaks and Is.

Beneath the stale stench of glitz, I smell an effluvium of natural flesh, a fresh waft of plant life, and, deeper, a scent of human seed that flares the girl's nostrils and tautens the folds of her jeans between her thighs; I let her lead me down the steps whose edges are lit with pink; the young detective leans his elbows upon the bar, speaks to the waitresses, one of whom—vase-shaped bust in black-and-pink lace, blond hair, big sad eyes, vague but searching—is paired with her reflection in the large mirror at her back, along with the face of the one who questions her and taps at his cigar; I don't dare to meet the girl's gaze at the same time as her hand tugs at mine and grazes my crotch till it's hot; the sensation radiates down to my knees; hunger hollows out my belly, as if my member were directly connected to my entrails—my desire to my will—in the need to eat from the deep, devour down to the hollow. The girl, at the bar, orders drinks and the detective pays for them; the wad of banknotes smells fresh; the remainder of my father's advance, forty days ago already? Bills crisp from the bank or payments for a day's work of house calls, drawn from the sugar tin on farmhouse tables or windowsills? Nausea catches me in the jaw... I go down into the basement: from a half-open toilet stall, a faint whimpering beneath wild laughter; a stockinged leg on which blood flows down to the high green heel and trickles onto the tiled floor: my gaze rises to the lurching chest, wrapped in shimmering silk—this body, fleshy, desiring, desired by what other body pressed against it in this cramped toilet stall, before my dazzled, blinking eyes? Halfway up the body, above where the blood oozes, a stench rises, not so much of excrement as of rotting entrails, a swarming of matter from one tube to another, from one gluey duct to another, incessant chemical transmutations, twisted black pudding in which the finest and most poignant delicacies—nursling calves—turn to stink over the course of their digestion, until they are defecated and decontaminate themselves as dung... it is our benevolence, our dread of being found to lack it, the shallowness of our urgency for life, our desire, that clothe these monstrous inner parts in beauty—just as we see fullness in an aggregate of atoms, art in a muddle of thought and form brought into some fixed arrangement. The human bodies we have today would have been conceived differently by our Creator; the bodies we bear are a fragile, naive, handmade assemblage—nothing for us, believers or unbelievers, to go into raptures over: "the perfection of the human body" is brought low by sex, surgical operations, pain, war, several million times per second, throughout the world.

Sophie

AUTUMN, Latin Quarter, I descend to the basement lodgings of a friend who has offered to type up my pages from the summer; at the back of the room beneath the cellar window that looks out onto the street—legs and feet of passersby, the Solex wheels and kickstand—at the end of a sofa on a pile of shawls and a load of unwashed underwear, a girls sits, her head cast back against the sofa cushion, her legs folded up between her haunches and the velvet, feet bare, hips in a short black skirt, breasts peeking from her red blouse each time she yawns... my friend, short, dark-haired, thick lips, straightens himself up; at the end of summer, when the first leaves fell and chestnuts tumbled loudly from the trees, I lost my desire to "get ahead" in the courier business, to make a career for myself there (an agency, with partners?), to forget about writing, to have done with the imagination.

And so, in my garret room at the hotel, I took up again the pages I'd written in Lyon, before my escape: fragments of memories of minor events in which our mother appears and speaks, and I asked my father, with whom I was now reunited, to read them, at home, on the red sofa beneath the large wall hanging from the Tatra Mountains: in these scenes traversed by our mother, where I linger on her intimate gestures, known to us alone, to him alone, I saw his eyes rise to my face and dim with tears as I sat before him and he said: "How do you know these things which are so true?"; I glanced quickly at what I had written further on and gently took the pages away from him, fearing he might suffer if he found I had possibly trespassed the unspoken limits of the knowledge a son may have of his mother; but, in seeing that the first texts I had consciously written as prose revived our dead mother, he was reassured of the strength of my filial affection.

The girl—petite, everything about her is flesh, even her clothing, nothing clothes her—lowers her head now toward her breast; I see her face, full cheeks, full eyes, full mouth, full ears hemmed by radiant hair; a bit of her nape quivers—from what yoke of my friend's, night and day, as they lie coupled?—she raises her eyelids, looks at me, tawny iris, her head inclined to the side: my heart stabs at me. He takes the pages, rolls a sheet into the machine, and begins to type; I come to his side, look at the handwritten text and the typed words; she stands up with a yawn, comes up behind me, leans, and looks, with her chin on my shoulder: it's the story of the little refugee child who arrived at our house to take shelter from the imprecise, murderous bombardments of Saint-Étienne in May 1944, classmates and teachers dead in the rubble; her breath along my cheek, her palm now grasps my shoulder; the tip of her breast presses against the edge of my back where my heart pounds, not from the text but from her... I turn my head, peer into the dark for the open bed whose scent I smell; he types and scratches his chest beneath the undershirt: What is she to him? A one-night one-day girl? She leaves my back; I feel cold there; she goes to the far end of the room, fills a saucepan with water from a jug, lights a thin gas flame beneath it; her movements generate heat in the cold room; the typed words fill the entire page; the boy's fright as he startles awake at night and runs in tears to the toilet, preceded by the stream of his piss. The words "our mother" appear at the end of the page; hunger pricks my belly.

With the couture shop closed for expansion and the regular couriers returned from vacation, I've been changing jobs every week or three days as a temp. Currently, I prepare envelopes for a company in Montrouge. At La Bonne Auberge on Place Saint-Michel, it isn't possible for me to trade up from my usual one-franc-thirty-centime set menu and order instead the one-franc-seventy-centime set menu (unchanged in price for years), of which, though it is richer in soup and hash browns, I would still need at least three to feed my tall nineteen-year-old frame; and I have already begun to avoid, on my daily routes, those streets at the entrance of which I can sniff the vapors of rotisseries; at night, if a bad dream awakes me, I eat bread, that ration so precious to the children of the war and yet still mediocre at present, too salty, halfway between black bread and white. My new friends, all of them students, can eat their fill nearby on Saint-Germain, take second helpings as they please, with free bread.

The friend—as the girl comes and goes in the darkness—I can feel his flesh and head heat up: scarce presences at their university classes, do they make love night, day, morning, afternoon, evening? Everything here is open, readied for embracing; everything is steeped in it, stained with it, the ceiling fogged with it; even their clothes, half-open, buttons and clasps a quarter undone. The piping-hot tea steams in the communal cup we pass to each other from mouth to mouth; she, as her large fresh eyes linger on mine, presses her thigh against the elbow of the friend, who finishes typing up the page and, mouth shimmering with tea, smiles at me and lowers his lashes toward the sofa: I know nothing and I know everything, except the thing I need to know; as she takes the cup from my lips and hands it to him, she draws her plump hand across the opening of my shirt at the top of my chest, touches the hairs there with her nail; he stands, pushes the pile to the other end of the sofa, stretches himself out, shorts full, taut, legs open and loose, wrists and hands behind his neck; he lights a cigarette, his large lips hold back the tip of his tongue; he lays a hand on the worn seat, taps there; her hand slips over my front, one of her breasts pokes out of her short sweater worn into holes at the armpit, she lowers her hips, steps back, turns around and crouches by the sofa; he, with a fling of his arm, takes her by the nape of the neck, and with his other hand designates the rest of the seat for me... I step back toward the far end of the room, the darkness, relight the gas beneath the saucepan: No one shall touch with outer lips my member—the seat of my boldness, and would not inner lips sap its strength, like Samson deprived of his hair...? But the more I push her away, the more I want her; and he, what's he whispering in her ear? The last words he typed, "our mother"—what's he doing with those words now, behind that low forehead of his where, as I watched in a barroom mirror one night a month ago, I saw him roll his wrinkles at three middle-aged men at a table, while a girl outside made eyes at them from the street.

Does she only want me with him as well, wanting me to want her since he wants me? And am I, all at once, in real life, to discover the orifices of both sexes and what to do with them?

Too cold outside and already too dark to set out again, seed wasted on something other than my clandestine nocturnal text—not my manifest text, of broad daylight, cold-worked—my belly empty, and the two of them, what pleasure could I possibly have given them beyond what they already take from each other; she who is said to have already been injured by a spoon-handle abortion?

Outside, hauling my Solex which has run out of gas, I wander through the neighborhood, taking streets I thought I'd already taken, my life before this moment shattered now or leading at every turn to her: her dimpled voice, her chest, her haunch, her good health, her anything-goes morals, the fourth of eight children—seduce all seven to get her?... —her mutilation—whose fetus if not the friend's?—her unconcern for things of the spirit—setting the cup down brusquely atop the trestle table where the friend was working, she pushed back the manuscript which soaked up tea and crinkled at the spot where the viper Athalia undulates outside her hole, raises her red-green body—everything about her attracts me, I see her everywhere or see her absence. At dinner, alone, I am compensated for the lack of the more expensive menu by the vision of her breasts poking beneath the threadbare wool riddled with even more holes than I saw on her; every form, living or inert, reminds me of her—the curves of banisters, cars, fruit, rounded clouds—every moving thing moves toward her, around her. Beauty, thought, world tragedies lose themselves in her, in her flesh, in her brain made of seductive flesh. All the girls and very young women I see outdoors or indoors, those saints, sinners, mystics, martyrs, spouses, shepherdesses, scullery maids, slatterns of church paintings—every one of them looks like her or doesn't look like her; at every girl's voice, I turn around—in vain—every little girl prefigures her... every space before me—alleyway, metro, turnstile, ticket window, bus—I want them all to be filled with her.

At the cinema, she—sitting between him and me—warm in the scent and breath of his sperm, sways her hip toward mine beneath the armrest, touches me lightly, pulls away; his neck is marked with her lipstick: Tomorrow? Where? I'll lay my hand on her and the rest will follow; I'll cross over into real life.

The Casket

THE SNOW glistens in the sun on the sill of the window I've opened to listen for my father's departure as he starts on his house call to assist a woman giving birth at a farm in the nearby Haute Loire. Two days after Christmas: I'm to return to Paris tomorrow, to her, to my hopes—to my hunger; precipitously, after lunch, I saw to it that everyone, my brothers and sisters, left the apartment, the house, and its approaches, so I might find myself alone there, between fear and laughter; I enter my parents' old bedroom where my father no longer wants to sleep; the sun fills it with its rays which warm me, quiet my trembling, envelop and approve my intent. The bed where our mother suffered, suffocated, and lay dying—where she let out her death rattle in August in front of us all as we stood at our father's side—is just as it was when her body was lifted from it after we had retired to the "daughters' room" at the back of the apartment to weep with our hands on our father's shoulders—and sob with laughter at the hats ferrying flowers and tufts of feathers on the heads of the visitors.

The white lace between the drawn curtains stirs a little from so much noonday sun penetrating it—before her body was lifted away, one fly and then three set themselves down on her wrinkles, until the sudden arrival of the porters made them take flight and knock against the ceiling—I open the armoire whose interior is unknown to me but my hand is sure, rummages beneath the linen over a locked drawer, feels for a little ring of little keys, opens with one of them the drawer where the brass cashbox lies: I take it, set it down on the bed, and

THE CASKET · 27

open it with the second key, smaller, golden. The church, the top of which shines beyond the window against the dark mass of the mountain covered in fir and chestnut trees, tolls the quarter hour; my heart beats more slowly than usual; I lift the cover: the wads of banknotes—set aside for the week's expenses?—lie there; except in the cash drawers of the wholesalers and semi-wholesalers and shopkeepers I served during my months as a courier, I've never seen so much private money; I slip two fingers under the bottom wad of banknotes, not fastened, and tug: a two-hundred-franc bill, enough to order the one-franc-seventy-centime menu for twelve days straight; I put the wads of banknotes back into place, shut the cashbox, slip it back under the linen. With the shopping all done by our sisters and us this morning, and me returning to Paris tomorrow morning, there is no reason the cashbox should be opened again until I am already out of reach. I go back up to my room under the eaves, resume work there on a text in progress for several voices, go down to walk in the snow, go back up to work: a day without work is a day of death; my conscience reproaches me for it, as it reproaches me for going to dinner without having produced.

Toward evening, I hear my father come back from his house calls, my brothers and sisters from the places I sent them. I pack my bag, go downstairs for dinner; on the stairhead, I hear from outside that someone has opened the empty bedroom whose window now lies open to the sounds from outdoors, the quarter hour ringing from the church. I step into the hallway; the boiler growls there; in the living room, my father stands holding the back of an armchair; my brothers and sisters are seated on the sofa; I enter. Our eldest sister, who keeps the accounts, says that there is money missing from the cashbox; that in looking for the sum she needed to pay for a final errand at the grocer's, she counted the wad of unfastened banknotes and a bill is missing; we all look at each other, but she and my father pretend to look at me less, their gaze slips over me and lingers on our youngest brother who has been in my charge since our mother's death; outside, the snow falls thick in the night; the vehicles spin their wheels on the ice. Anger rises in my muscles, my blood: they know it's me, because for a long time now I have provoked suspicion—running away from home, writing in secret, believing in my destiny.

But they must make a show of equity, a few paces away from the empty room—whose sacred space, too, I may have violated; but didn't she, her shadow, watch me from the bed as I took what I would need, in Paris, to eat better? And would she have disapproved?

When I eat the basic menu, in the cigarette smoke and steam of cooking pots, isn't she, a spirit, there on my shoulder, whispering to me that I'm in the right, that I'm on the straight and narrow path?

Why seek to know who stole? Instead, so soon after a feast day, a reconciliation, the second one without her whose corpse now lies decomposing in the frozen ground nearby on our massif's southern slope, we should all embrace each other, fulfill each other's needs, support our lonely father; wouldn't our eldest brother, a soldier in Algeria, my companion in painting and music—he who, long ago, as a little schoolboy in his cape, was hardened to hunger during the Occupation—wouldn't he laugh at this pointless tribunal?

Until midnight, the questions, coercions encircle me, assault me; I want to escape to the mountain and hold out until dawn... my father holds me back firmly by the shoulders; we are alone in the living room now; I lift an armchair aloft, advance toward my father who shields himself with his arm, I brandish the armchair over him: "You would strike your own father?" Could it be that they predicted my theft? Did they vacate the premises deliberately to allow me to commit it here? And thereby—through my confession and contrition, my submission—to obtain my reintegration into the family order so that, furnished with an allowance from my father, I might resume my studies? All of them, accomplices in this show? My two youngest brothers? Exhausted, each of them, as I am, by this agony, bone-weary in their young limbs.

Until dawn—hold out until morning to escape forever, in broad daylight, by way of the north or the south—we remain face to face, retreating or advancing from one end of the room to the other, seated or standing, according to our grievances in the diminishing shadow.

At dawn, after yet another accusation and his demand that I give back the banknote, as I stand up and say I will never come back again, my father kneels before me, begs me not to leave him here alone; I collapse into his arms, him risen to his feet again, he lays me down on the sofa, takes my pulse; I burn with fever and tremble; his scent of ether and cigarillos—he stopped smoking when our mother's sickness was first diagnosed, and started again after her death—wafts its fragrance over my return from the fainting fit; his shadow rests upon me as in days of old it rested upon us children as we fell asleep after our prayers.

The morning bus for Saint-Étienne honks outside beneath the snow-covered chestnut trees: I give back the banknote, get my bag from upstairs, come down, legs unsteady, nausea in my throat; outside, I run through the snow toward the bus; my father stands at one of the living-room windows; his hand rises up behind the glass. The telephone calls resume in the entrance hall; the snow too; a night without sleep, the ruts, the snowdrifts, the ice... but he knows every tree, every crag, and the husbands or fathers or brothers come from the farms and take his satchel or doctor's bag, and guide him out from the car, through the snow squall...

A few women get off at the third stop in the mountains; a few chickens cackle in baskets; here, a man lives in hiding who, in his youth, betrayed a Resistance cell of Polish communist adolescents that the Germans massacred in a clearing.

I contain my anger, stronger than my sense of deliverance, to keep myself from a stronger nausea; the scent of the snow, of coffee in the farmhouses, of cow dung, does nothing to appease it.

On the train to Paris, where I will arrive late in the evening, as I see the villages, towns, small cities bustling under the snow, people in the stations embracing, my anger fades and little by little—but the worst is yet to come—remorse takes complete hold of me as I hop from the train at Gare de Lyon; as I cross the Pont d'Austerlitz to reach my rooming house on the Montagne Sainte-Geneviève, the cold crystallizes my remorse; the shame is in my bones; a man who tumbles from such a bridge and is drowning and whom the firemen haul from the turbulent waters thick with ice and mud and wood is more forthright with the world than I am; all my secrets, all my failings flow before my conscience older than original sin itself, threaten to disintegrate it. Everything I can remember, about myself, about others, about those I've loved, admired, every tragedy of the world, everything I see before me at this instant, is marked by my theft; redo yesterday morning, different: the bedroom stays shut; the sinking sun casts its beams there beneath the door; me under the eaves, making my figures speak; after lunch I go down and accompany my father to a low farmhouse, snowdrifts as high as the roof, merry red-cheeked children, wooden clogs tapping on dirt floors, the grandmother warms black coffee and herself, too, there at the edge of the hearth; my father, upstairs, lifts the sheet over a woman giving birth; my father starts out again in the night to the edge of town, to set the broken bones of an adolescent who has crashed his sled into a tree trunk hidden beneath the snow; we all write letters, play cards, listen to the radio and to our 78s and our few LPs; redo the previous days up to yesterday, extinguish all the fits of anger in them, diminish the fear of hunger in them, cover them all in vivid text, shake them up with some skiing, offer them up in liturgy; the people I pass beneath the streetlamps know of my theft, they can see it; must I, yet again, pull the bell rope at the foot of the hotel beneath Saint-Étienne-du-Mont where I have my garret room under the eaves overlooking the Tour Saint-Jacques? Bid Happy New Year to the parsimonious hotelkeepers, open my mouth, force words from my throat, climb the stairs, take the key from my pocket, open the room? Immediately, the room before my departure, before my fault, appears to me, tidy—but, at nearly twenty years of age, what do I have to tidy away there except what I have on me, stuffed in the little backpack whose buckles I struggle to unfasten for all my trembling. Lie down in this ghost? Draw back the bedclothes? Slip my rigid body into it, forbidden to move a limb? Fall asleep there, give free rein to dreams?

I am forced to control, with my exiled reason, all the acts that nature causes to be done naturally.

The following morning, I don't turn on the radiator: Dare an act of comfort, as if I were alive?

I go out and walk: let my steps through the cold lead me where my corpse would lead me.

And even so, carcass, skeleton, do I have the right? More rigid than a skeleton, to appear before the Creator who, alone, could cause my bones to move again, cause my blood to spring through my veins again?

Not Christ, too inclined to forgive when my shoulder would resist his pierced hand.

I lost myself before the spirit of the holy one today as I watched God, felt His touch: no moral fault, but a fault of order, a departure from His logic, a mere nothing of a sacrilege and yet a lifelong death; and an offense against the earthly father. Why has He forsaken me? I know my turpitudes: Does He know of yet another within me, worse and unknown to me, that makes Him abandon me to theft? Why, in the room filled with light as from an apparition of His son, did He fall silent within me, once my decision was made? Why didn't He strike me down with lightning, me, clasping the stolen banknote, burn me and burn the banknote with me? I am struck down with lightning, but alive; colder than the cold that encompasses me.

Return to my room and suffer there in a closed space, the manuscript from before the Fall lying closed on the table: Pick up the pen again, believe, hope, let speaking figures unbind my tongue?

Hungry, and pained by this need that makes me feel alive, binds me to others whose lives, even if guilty, are pure and untouched by this offense, this crime, I enter a bakery: the heat catches me in the face, the scent of the bread oven calls me back to my ancestors, of whom I have made myself unworthy: to my maternal great-great-grandfather, a mystic and baker in the Croix-Rousse district of Lyon during the Restoration. The fragrance of the baker's breasts, her tender and scolding voice, make me flee; in what cold place, without voice or gaze, can I buy what I need to hold out for a day?

At an automat, I buy some bread, peanut oil, and salt, and take it to my room, which is no longer an honest abode but a makeshift hovel where I, unworthy animal, stash my winter provisions; the hotelkeeper, whom I cannot avoid, is surprised both that I am bringing food into her establishment where it is forbidden and that I am now eating so little. Bite, chew, dip the bread in the bowl of oil, add salt; movements, gestures wrenched from this great privation, which is not a voluntary act of contrition or even a fact of my poverty, but seems to have descended from the sky—a sky that I no longer see, whether by day or by night, and whose memory does evil to me where it remains in the remnants of my inward recitations of poetry; but this evil is equal to good; there is neither evil nor good, nothing beyond myself—but what self?—except other people, glorious or wretched, foul or fragrant, distant in time or near.

Every gaze that settles upon me—upon my gaze—is a gaze upon someone else, to the side, behind, far in the distance even: I no longer exist. How, no longer existing, can I live? I no longer see my friends. If I spot one of them waiting for me outside the hotel—to recognize him or her as a friend would give me an identity again, which I don't want—I step back behind the doorway. I no longer pass through our usual haunts except late at night; to go home to sleep is to go home to die; I am unworthy even of dying.

Places, objects, natural facts observed and loved before the theft, clouds, snow, bridges, river, statues, facades of buildings—everything appears as if from an ancient world that my offense prevents me from experiencing even as nostalgia. The metro leads me nowhere: west is the same as south; east the same as north; faces are shadows; voices, echoes.

Hunger, in the evenings, gnawed, devoured by itself; everything, gnawed at, swallowed up by the offense; thought impossible, the least inner word that issues forth, no sooner conceived than swallowed.

From day to day, to night, privation slows the pace of time, space; hunger makes me walk faster and faster; as I cross the street near the Palais-Royal, a big car hits me, knocks me down; I clasp my hands, my head beneath the hood of the car; I get back up; go off down an adjacent street, gaze at a shop window; only when I cross the street again at the same place do I feel the impact of the collision; people sitting on a terrace remind me that I was just hurt in an accident there; I only hear sounds as before-sounds or after-sounds; distances are diminished, and my haste to cross through them intensifies my fatigue; that dome over there is in reach of my palm; when I see a child eat, I eat what he eats, what the whole family eats.

Passing a large concert hall, I hear, I listen to, through a basement window shut by the snow, piano arpeggios, glissandos of strings; I recognize the piece but I immediately thrust out from my inner vision the title page of the score, beheld many a time in a book, "before."

I wander through Paris, the immediate outskirts that I crisscrossed last summer on my errands for the bighearted seamstresses, my own heart so merry at the time. To the north, near the Zone, whose musty reek is not lessened by the snow, the carts of voiceless ragmen totter over icy cobblestones, dust, ash all around; hovels, flocks of mud-spattered children.

I am no longer writing; I will no longer write. I don't touch the scraps of cutlets in the restaurant rubbish bins but later, as I walk hunched against the cold, I chew in thought their scraps of flesh, which I can feel stuck between my teeth and which I pluck out with my nail; I gnaw at their bones.

From night to night, those things that stood in opposition to the annihilated present—the time before the theft up to the final minutes before my entrance into the dazzling bedroom, my childhood, my faith, my adolescence, my painting, my poetry—veil themselves, die out in a sniggering chastisement: heaps of ashes; I have to distract my thoughts from them or see to it that nothing of them remains, or even that nothing ever took place before I grasped the ivory latch.

My dreams? Formed of things from before. At least in dreams I lose my self of skin, of contours; is it truly "I" who experience them? Or do the things seek me out, seek a self within me? The nightmares from which I wrench myself sweating, feverish, teeth chattering, in tears sometimes, death rattle in my throat—I take them as a refusal to let dreams of travel, of tribunals, of love, confer an identity upon me again, and as I lay myself down to sleep I hope for them.

One black night, having walked too late too far in the southern outskirts to be able to return by public transportation, I lose my way in a construction zone where, farther on, among the unfinished buildings, a jut of concrete half covers a stream whose streaming I can hear beneath the ice. I step through what I see: worksite paths, wooden barriers, boards over trenches; step through them again in the opposite direction; dogs in the distance bark at a line of flashing lights in the sky; my scarf catches on barbed wire at neck level, my fingers get tangled there, my breath fogs my lenses; I move forward; in a half-demolished building, I climb what remains of the steps to a three-room roofless entresol where the passage of a low-altitude plane casts a little light: I enter, hands stretched before me; in one of the rooms covered in wallpaper that hangs from the crumbling plaster, I grope through the darkness, my shin knocks against a bed that I edge my way around: one of its legs is missing; a red coverlet spangled with ice, a blue-striped pillow, the fragrance of a woman, an intact mattress on which I stretch myself out; in the inside pocket of my jacket I have a heel of bread that, tilting my head to the side, I gnaw on beneath the coverlet until I fall asleep.

Cries awaken me; I look bare-eyed toward the cries, shrill, hoarse, all the louder in that they sound as if they are sent forth from a little throat, from what will become a little throat, as when I was a child sitting in the farmhouse downstairs beside the hearth at the grandmother's side, I heard the first cry of a newborn child that my father upstairs was helping into the world; to see, I need my glasses; I put them on; I cough, my lungs are feverish; between the leafless branches of a shrub, I see lights flicker, flash from the facade of a large new white building, from one bay window to the next, on the upper floors; are the windows half-open, for these repeated cries to pass through? A newborn? Two? Twins from the same mother? Several newborns from several mothers in several rooms? Lights turn on in rows and on other floors, above, below: Births by the row? Cries on every story? Parturitions at the same hour, at the same minute? Parturient women from here and elsewhere gathered together, night by night, from here to there, in the same oblong block where I can already hear the workers, their hammers and trowels, finishing their construction; hatchery, ship of lives to come. The planes, reappearing in the black dawn, bring in mothers, carry away newborns...

I come out from under the ice-cold coverlet; I stagger in the shafts of light, along the watercourse that carries reddened scraps, rags, placentas tracked by barking dogs, toward a stretch of paved road where other people are walking, muffled up; we walk toward what appears to be a bus shelter in front of which a chiming vehicle stops; everyone climbs in, I hide myself among their overcoats, my smell among theirs; the bus drives toward Paris, enters the city; is this really Paris? Have we moved at all since the frozen stream? I go on foot to my hotel, climb to my garret room, eat a piece of crust dipped in oil from the bottle that I hide at the bottom of my backpack with the box of salt, since food is forbidden in the rooms.

Washed, I go back down to walk; my foot on a patch of ice summons me to before the theft; every armoire at the back of an antique shop summons me to the room where I was born and where I stopped my life; they, over there, even if tormented, are among the living.

Even he, my father—but is he still?—so solitary, wronged, and by my hand.

In street, shop, room, I hesitate to touch the things from my life before, from the lives of others: Do I have the right? The knob of a gate at the Tuileries Garden, a metro ticket, coins; can I, in a church, gaze at a statue's gaze, at the gaze of a face in a painting? My gaze, bare-eyed or with my glasses, flits over the small light of the Holy Sacrament in the tabernacle: no god watches over me now. Who is it who willed me, begot me, birthed me? Was I even? Or could I be a double, rejected by its original? I attempt to find a vantage point upon myself, to see myself in all that I remember of the stream of my young life, and everything collapses as my inner eye approaches the moment of the theft: the act, committed in broad daylight, cannot be hidden from the panorama of my inner gaze. No act of Good, or even an act of fatal heroism, can ever blot it out. And my outer eyes remain dry: no remorse, no punishment can abolish the offense; there is no friendly hand—the only one now rots beneath the earth—to touch my hand or shoulder and...

No mouth—the only one (and is that even sure?) now opens into teeth, into bone, in the grave beneath the concrete slab—to touch my cheek, my brow, my nape: that motion she made so often, suddenly embracing me from the side and rubbing my back, would be the motion, now, of a skeleton, oh god!

I cross streets, avenues, squares without looking to the right or left or in front of me, as if I didn't exist, neither to myself nor to others: the braking cars, the blaring horns, are for the living. At best, my torment at no longer being a full self hinders external movement—like a pillar of stone; a salt pillar of unshed tears.

I return to my room late at night; up there, I take out bread, oil, salt, open the door again, look out onto the landing, down the staircase, for fear that one of the hotelkeepers, she or he, will come up to listen for my eating. I leave the door open; their ascending shadow would appear on the wall of the downstairs landing. I slowly uncork the bottle, slowly pour the oil into the bowl, dip the soft middle of the bread without knocking against the sides of the bowl, shake the box of salt. I eat the crust without making it crackle—I'll eat the heel, harder, tomorrow, during the hotelkeeper's noisy housework.

In the dead of night, I get up, go down to piss in the Turkish toilet on the floor below; as I come back up the stairs I see a gray silhouette, genderless, standing with its shoulder against the frame of my door; its empty eyes follow me as I brush past it and enter the room. I fall asleep, encounter the silhouette again in one of my dreams, but big-breasted or big-balled, depending on the scene; in the morning, as the rays of sunlight make the open manuscript disappear from the table in their dazzling brilliance, the silhouette, genderless again, slips away toward the half-open door, passes through it; I hear a snickering on the staircase, an upstairs neighbor laboring a difficult defecation.

I walk in the snow rather than on cleared ground, to make less noise: do not wake the pain. I follow the carts of ice blocks that horses draw from one bistro to the next, but the smell of their dung in the smell of the snow pricks my heart, the smell of the places where my father, bundled up in his shearling coat, walks toward the farmhouses.

One day at noon, as I follow a lean-flanked dog that wags and whines for me—what more could I give him than one of my last heels of bread, or should I lead him to one of the streets of eating houses in the intellectual quarter where, after a short lazy morning, everyone gathers to eat lunch at the expense of their masters: Rummage in the back kitchens there?—I enter a little street of low houses where, last autumn, I saw her, S., letting the hand of someone other than her regular man lift her short light-wool sweater, nearly worn through at the nipples, her eyes raised, rolled back into her head, in the half-light of the doorway papered with green-and-red posters for the Algerian insurrection: at the time, mere contact with this sign was as good as complicity. I step to the now bare wall, sniff its scent in the frozen air: her haunch rubbed against this plaster, her fresh cheek, round, the same as the cheeks of her seven sisters and brothers whose group photo she showed me to dissuade me from loving only one, her alone... her breasts touched here when he turned her around to clutch her from the back. It is from someone other than me that my member raises itself; do I still have a soul? Was it taken from my body along with my honor?

The dog, half my heel of bread devoured, lick-drinks the snow, wags its thick tail, licks my hand, trots farther on. I follow him; other dogs join him, join us, wander off, scuttle away, right, left, gather into a pack again far ahead of us, past the Pont Neuf: the pack scatters among the Baltard Pavilion, but the dog nudges at my legs and licks my hands to lead me toward the meat stalls; the snow begins again, heavy and wet in the night; am I not as famished as this dog, whose jaws, throat, bowels, rectum can accommodate themselves to street waste? And if he snatched me a cutlet from a market stall, all they could do is beat his flanks as he ran away or crept or leapt into some inaccessible place; but me, if I did the same, I'd be seized, thrown into a cell, judged, condemned. Make him seize a cutlet for me from a stall? Theft, even more theft, even more nonexistence. And eat it gnaw it raw? Roast it over some wretched fire in a doorway of wretched people, take from them some of the fire that warms them? Where to hide and eat it once it was seized, dripping with its fat? Farther on toward the wasteland of Beaubourg? On the quay? At the entrance to the Rue Saint-Denis, the dog, raw cutlet clamped in his fangs, leaves me: Are my fingers, my mouth, smeared with fat? For in the silent movement of men through the snow, one, two, three dogs brush against me as if to lick it off.

From a red corridor, white-corseted breasts come toward me under neon light; I feel myself grow pale, my teeth hold back an empty retching, my bowels writhe, my mouth writhes with pain, the rumblings of my stomach echo in the padded corridor, the breasts move, leap before the falling snow; I stifle with my fists this rumbling that betrays me: a blast of hot air makes my limbs grow slack, I see above the breasts a ringleted head whose mouth opens to the snow, calls to me as flakes melt on the pursed lips; gather all my strength in flesh, muscle, and bone to fling me from this red lechery! The plump hand beneath her breasts grazes my thigh, my hollowed stomach; I slip on the pavement that's covered in ice again, get up, backside bruised; the shock, the pain, stops my swoon; I walk, coughing in fits, hobbling, toward Saint-Eustache—formerly the church of Saint Agnes, virgin martyr brought to a brothel and then, after hair had sprouted over her entire inaccessible body, slit at the throat—where figures in rags step from the porch stairs.

Rue du Jour

COULD it be Sunday? A benediction of the Holy Sacrament is being prepared far in the high nave illuminated at the back: the monstrance, the rustling of chasubles, flights of the altar boys' albs, and the smell of incense, metal, precious fabrics: a hymn begins haltingly from the left side of the choir next to the sacristy; trembling, I sit down on a fixed chair in one of the rows near the vestibule to the left of the Chapel of the Redemption; the heat rises up along the pillar; I unbutton the large jacket that covers my blazer, but the dizziness catches hold of me again along with the coughing that worsens it; to my right, where vertigo keeps me from turning my head to look directly, I can make out a table lit up with burning candles, the edges overhung with wax... already, from the choir, the Salutaris Hostia, children's throats, wafts of incense; behind me, beneath the great organ, one of the padded double doors opens, shuts; a woman's perfume moves quickly toward the candles whose flames gutter low; the parishioners before the choir aren't a Sunday crowd: longshoremen, market porters, truckers, stallkeepers, in their work clothes, girls... could it be the feast of Saint Agnes, and therefore also the feast day of our Agnès, our grandmother's little part-time maid, blond, fresh-faced from the up-mountain farms, who unbuttoned her rosy breasts for me by the corridor sink for her saint's feast day, the 21st of January? So for more than twenty days I've wandered through the city, less than an outcast, subsisting on bread and oil and salt; beheaded like Louis XVI on this same day; the edge of the sword that slit the virgin Agnes's throat in the bawdy house, seconded by the guillotine's civic blade, presses against my throat, a shadow on the paving stone redoubles the perfume.

Is this the same girl, barely a woman, whom I saw up close last summer beneath the neon sign in front of a red staircase, when I came near and caught scent of her with Laideronette at my side, her perfume holding out at the time against the reek of meat from Les Halles raw beneath the flies, the reek of sweat, the breath of men in rut? Arm held high, armpit hair glistening, her lifted hand dipping and motioning to the last man in the line, a fresh bare-chested worker hitching up his string-belted pants with his fist.

Cast out this image that makes me have a past! A white fur jacket appears to my right, obscures the lights of the votive candles; high on a woman's shoulders, the worn hairs graze the little flames; a hand, plump, familiar with folds, holes, interstices, its supple fingers moving independently, grasps a candle firmly; the other hand slides a coin into the slit of the cashbox; the tinkling summons the memory of a gold coin briefly glittering at the bottom of the cashbox in the armoire—as does every sound, since the theft, of cash registers in shops. The little hand sticks the new candle onto the spike; the fingers near the wick uncap a golden lighter, strike the flint: the flame lights up a face whose makeup has been removed but the cheek still sticks to the fur a little as it turns; a very fine scar—does she unstitch her skin in the act of love?—runs from the middle of her upper lip, onward beneath her slightly upturned nostril, along the plane of her cheek, to underneath the bare ear where a spot of dried blood shines on the lobe; my gaze remains fixed on this cheek that pulses with inner speech: a vow, a hope, a fit of rage, or what I dare not think of, some detailed act of the trade, recent or still to come.

Where can I lie down at full length? A silhouette entering through the little white-wood antechamber door at the south end of the church pushes cold air toward the choir, wafts the parishioners' sweat and smell of viands toward my nostrils: What would I vomit after eating nothing but bread and rancid peanut oil for three weeks, the digestion of which I defecate only in the middle of the night, in the anguish of dawn? The little flames gutter toward the vestibule beneath the great organ behind me. Are her breasts hanging bare-skinned beneath the fur that advances alongside me? A light blouse catches and covers the breasts up to the beginning of the neck; the nipples, thick—but what do I know at the time about girls' nipples in real life, beyond photos, films, paintings? I've never touched one with my fingers, much less with my mouth, but long ago, unaware, body at liberty, I touched and sucked my mother's—rise ever so slightly from the fabric. Her dress is larger, not as short as the one she wore in summer, the flowers are stretched on the cloth that hugs her loins, moist between her thighs: sweat? Piss from a baby or a little child?—Does she have one that she leaves with a wet nurse and who, at the joy of feeling her touch, relieves itself on her knees?

She steps back to the side toward the votive candles—through my eyes that can no longer see anything but striped dazzles of light, through my ears where the buzzing begins again, along with my father's supplication on his knees and the drone of the great organ—I see and hear how she limps a little; turning my head even slightly brings the vertigo on again. Her brow beneath the little reddish-blond curls is knobbed like the forehead of one who fights till dawn—I'm quick to imagine, as my heartbeat spikes, that her curls are blond but sullied by the way she burrows between the thighs of all comers at their command. Her nape—she turns around, her high heels creaking, toward someone who has just come in from the vestibule or stepped down from the organ—is tender on sturdy bone: made for hands, for lips, for the yoke that it submits to but resists, that it breaks to pieces; made for the world to weigh heavy upon, to rest there on the downy blond hairs whose sweat scintillates in the flattened unsteady gleam of the candles: this neck so often lying between the legs of all and sundry—male and female?—if the session lasts long, or locked in the elbow of the pimp, the girl-merchant; my eyes grow dim and drift away from her to the mystic flesh of the paintings hanging in the chapels, to the marble, plaster, gilded-wood flesh of kneeling angels: enter now, what's left of my spirit, heart, bone, muscles, sinews, into this flesh half-naked or draped in folds or coats of skins; look through their eyes, pray through their clasped hands, wings sprouting from my shoulders...Who is it who prays behind this open-worked wood? A Princesse de Lamballe, loyal to her queen, silly, brave girl whose murderers will soon make for themselves a bloody mustache of her cut, torn sex...but as for this girl here, the little one whose breasts now swing to and fro to the tapping of her tall heels: When a male shoves his howling market-crier face into her sex, doesn't he blink his eyes at her above the flat of her wretched womb, with the upturned hairs of her shared sex against his lips? The sound of the sucking fills my ear: quick (break the spell), go back to the idea I have been pursuing since the chilly outdoors, as I sit on this wicker chair, with hot and cold sweat on my brow and hands, without reaching a conclusion: a straight and level idea at last, all adjacent distractions cast aside, an idea of Being—human, animal, nature, object—as my habitual thought digs, pushes like a dung beetle pushing its dung; think all things at once, forge ahead in even the smallest idea with all my being, when my habitual thought persists in its stubbornness or leaps up and loses itself high up in History. My edge-of-the-abyss thought falls headlong now, at the thought of my mother decaying in the frozen ground under the blue winter sky, at the thought that she would have had, seated alive at my side, at this thought, my own, accompanying it, rocking it to its fulfillment, impossible on Earth, possible in her hereafter, the shadow of which surrounds me. And I have not yet lived enough to think the thought of Being.

Quick, think, fix my thought on some object, inert, whole, commonplace! But everything, the back of the chair in front of me, tip of my shoe, cracked paving stone, uncracked paving stone, foot of a chair, cigarette ash on the ground—everything leads to more thoughts, just as much as the girl's perfume, the music, and the light of the paintings behind me, or the little bells of the Benediction drawing to an end far off in the golden glare; how to put off my fainting? If I close my eyelids, it's for life: the darkness seizes me, nothingness dissolves me alive; if I fall, it's to death—and the piss and worse beneath me on the paving stone; and my corpse unidentified—after the theft, I threw away my card—alone in this vast, ancient city, more than two thousand years old, and how many millennia still to come? Lie down at full length on the ground—do I still have enough time and strength? Set three chairs together and lie back on them?

The noise I make as I do so—for the chairs are fixed to each other—rouses something to my right: I can still see the flower-print fabric stretched between two hips, between two flanks on which the girl presses her worker hands in the street, the candlelight on her wrist, and her dimpled chin and the pleasure folds of fat around her neck; I try to stand up, come out from the row, bend my knees, kneel down, lie flat on the paving stones where muddy snow is melting; I see nothing now but darkness, my brow sinks into a footprint of snow, takes in the coolness there...

The sound of plates, forks and spoons, mouths chewing, wakes me long enough to sense that I am lying warm in a pair of pajamas; my eyelids remain shut; the darkness seizes me again with a nausea that pitches my cheek onto a cool pillow...

A palm passes before my eyelids, which open a little; a strong hand grasps mine beneath the coverlet; I see a large watch emerge from a waistcoat pocket; I hear an elderly voice but not the words, sink back to the darkness, then feel a tapping on the upper part of my formless body; a thin yellow light passes through my crusted lashes; a sweet liquid through my teeth; a door grates on its hinges, slams shut; a plump hand caresses my brow; long-nailed fingers pass through my abundant hair, smooth the strands down, scratch my scalp; my mouth and cheeks stretch, crease for a smile that my principal organs, hardened, refuse.

I feel my toes stiff against the coverlet; my eyelids half open beneath fingers that rub a damp cloth there; a shaft of sun illumines and warms the white wrist; from beneath the coverlet, a hand, my own, still pale, rises and lays itself upon the wrist...

Later—for the sun is now red through the snow lying heavy on the skylight that my eyes, rolled up in a remnant of vertigo, see above me—a perfumed shape bends over my face; from her, fabric and flesh, a breast emerges; words that I cannot separate from each other sing from above; a nipple haloed in grayish red approaches my lips; little blue veins pulse on the globe of the breast; I smell the scent of milk there—a horse paws at the ground in the snowy street below; hitched to its milk cart? Should I cover the nipple with my moistening lips, open my teeth to it, lay the tip of my tongue on it? How to suckle? Go back to my earliest days, to my being, even preconscious, touch in thought this detested being that I keep at a distance, the better to target it in its entirety when the time comes? And what if my teeth were to close upon a void between bones? Did the doctor, whose odor of old age I smelled, recommend to her that she nurse me back to life with her milk? Who keeps her baby for her? What man is it from? Share this milk with the infant born of a mother whose bones creak day and night beneath the weight of all and sundry males in this enclosure of meat, fresh and rotting, where rats gallop about?

A drop of milk falls on the middle of my lips; a little laugh bursts out; farther away, the door of an armoire opens to an odor of naphthalene: Is she hiding her money there? Or, to judge by a clacking on the floor, under a tile?

Do I have the mark of the theft upon my brow, so that, even while giving me her breast, she would busy herself protecting her earnings from the wildness of my hand?

Again a golden light at the skylight, then red, then night: the elderly hand grasps mine again; a sound of crinkling paper, the same as I would hear in my father's palm when people—except the poorest ones—paid him for his house call or consultation; and my heart flies into a frenzy: Could he have come all the way here to take me back, to remake my being? But the hand is too bony; the veins too prominent.

Near the tolling of midnight at Saint-Eustache—count the strokes;

risk that my being returns as I do so—a coolness comes from the side of the room where the door has opened: skin, suit cloth, pâté, sea salt. Without my glasses I can see only blurriness, colors, hardly any forms except those a foot in front of my face; once again, the sound of plates and cutlery, but for more than just one person, a gas burner igniting, a boiling in which I smell potatoes; "I" want to sit up, but to prop myself on my elbows would be to regain my confidence in the world and reacquaint myself with shame and rage there. Voices, sounds of chewing, then the sound of a kiss, but familial, not carnal.

A sound of bedsprings toward what might be the back of the room that my eyes know only from the part that appears day and night above my head; a warm shape slips under the coverlet; I let it make itself comfortable at my side: Could this be the shape to which belong the smell and one of the voices I heard above the noise of the eating? Beneath the coverlet I can hear fingers undo a watch bracelet from a different wrist and place it on the ground where the bedstead stands or—for all I know as yet—the mattress lies straight on the tiles: the shape is naked; it smells naked; tender, sweet, attentive, it does not touch me but enfolds in fraternal warmth the parts of my body that has been remaking itself for perhaps three days now beneath the coverlet—chest, groin, thighs, knees, toes.

On the other side of the room, higher up than us, a sound like that of an elastic band snapping against firm flesh: Her bra, removed from her breasts? Lower down, an elastic band again, slipped off and releasing an odor.

I fall asleep on my left side; the shape falls asleep, rolling to its right; its legs spread a little but just as they are about to touch mine, my dream begins, a dream of breastfed bed rest from which I wake with a start, chest covered in sweat where my heart races, my mouth parched ... My hand comes out from under the coverlet, goes down, touches a little wicker stool where a ray of moonlight pierces the layer of melting snow atop the skylight and lights up my red glasses case. I open it, take out my glasses, put them on, turn toward the shape: a ringleted head, lit by its pale-blond hair, is pitched downward into empty space, its neck tendons taut, its mouth open for abrupt snores in which mucus rattles; a coffee mill creaks toward the back of the room behind our bed frame; the head yawns, lifts itself back on a level with the mattress; blue eyes blaze in the moonbeam which has taken on a tinge of violet; the same mouth as that of the girl; the same chin but without the pleasure fold beneath; the shape sits up straight; a hand pushes back the edge of the coverlet; a boy leaps up, hops onto the tiles, runs toward the smell of the coffee. Bones crackle; the standing embrace concludes in a violent kiss; the boy comes back to the bed, crouches before me naked except for navy-blue boxers, elbows at his knees, hands at his eyes, palms at his chin, face radiant; a swath of white peignoir moves beside his shoulder: it's her; I lift my eyes again, past the open placket where the warm breasts move, to her face: I see the scar there again; a mouth already made up over the remains of coffee smiles at me; slightly large teeth shine in the morning sun. The boy pulls the swath of white up to his weathered cheek, rubs against it; he stands up in a single movement; the girl rests her chin on his shoulder; he scratches at a pimple on his inner thigh; I see he has an erection, strong and high; he draws his hand up to his sighing chest; behind him is a bureau sculpted with wooden fruits and flowers: on top of it, among dolls, are two small picture frames inside metal arabesques: one shows the girl in communion dress holding the hand of a woman in a peasant's apron, flowers in the background; the other shows the boy in his first-communion clothes, a white band on his arm, hand in hand with another woman who is holding a pitchfork, the ground covered in straw. A little green stove roars near the door where his sailor's hat hangs with its ribbon and red pompon, and his navy-blue dress uniform on a coat hanger, with knee breeches and a white-collared peacoat.

Not yet able to stand, I am at their mercy and I burden their little space with my heavy, awkward body; my presence, even in this weakened state, disturbs their reunion; my theft, even though I have kept it secret, seeps through their chest of drawers, through their clothes, their intimate things, cutlery, plates, provisions, through their shelves of toiletries, ointments, beauty supplies, inside the very bottles, the jars, through the pockets of their clothes, through their billfolds, through their shoes. No gaze of mine can ever be candid again; no act of mine pure.

The girl steps out onto the stairhead to knock at the door of an old woman who lives alone, whom she says she checks on every morning to make sure she's alive, the old woman replying from her big, high bed under the eaves. The girl picks up a sparrow on the stairhead, frozen, legs in the air, and slips it onto my belly between the coverlet and my pajamas—who could have told her that I'm accustomed to taming animals? I fall asleep or pass out again: when I awake, the bird is moving in the hairs of my groin; the girl picks it up again, her wrist brushing against my member, gives it sugar water to drink, hempseed to eat; the bird hops on the oilcloth table cover; I try to get out from under the coverlet; as the boy returns from the half-darkness with scrubbed face and washed hair, my nostrils flare at the sweet odor of piss smelled as a child in the lodgings of the workers in our town—unmade beds, mewling urchins—still peasants until only recently. Does it come from his well-stuffed boxers? He bends to take me by the arm, then by the shoulder; she takes my other arm; one foot touches the floor tiles, then two; I stand up, stay on my feet; the sparrow lies flat on the oilcloth, wiggling its head upward with half-closed eyelids; the girl, holding me on my right, gives me a kiss on the right side of my neck; the boy, at my left, gives me a kiss on the left side; with the laughter of each in my ears, I walk at their side through the room whose darkened far end I discover: shelves of provisions, a hot plate, hanging dishes, laundry, a little tinplate sink; deeper inside, a vast bed sculpted with fruits and flowers; against the narrow wall, a mirror wardrobe that smells of underwear.

The sparrow has stopped moving; it's sleeping, wobbling a little. They sit me down at the table in a wicker armchair; the boy takes the sparrow, walks to the door, goes out onto the landing; I see him open the small window near the floor, unclench his fist; the sparrow clings to his fingers—is it shitting in his palm?

The girl sets out cups and a coffeepot on the oilcloth that covers the table at the edge of which a little account book lies open: the revenue of her trade? I glance at it sidelong: the figures in blue ink set my heart aflutter again, but with an old desire to write, and, in the pajamas of the brother, my member straightens out against my will—my "wild," clandestine writings are too much for it. Today, no longer alive, I harbor neither disgust nor shame toward them: all turpitude prior to the theft seems like child's play; the stove roars; the boy, crouching, still half-naked, robust haunch, loads it with kindling. The sparrow sleeps in a box of rags on the ground, lets out a little peep each time it wakes.

Washed, dressed—he in his uniform; she in her fur coat—they go out, me in bed again, coffee at my lips; where are my clothes? Leave? Run away? Scrawl a message in the notebook? The imprint of the brother's body alongside me smells of cinders, beer, salty sweat; I'm still too feeble to stand; did the doctor leave a prescription?

Noon tolls at Saint-Eustache, staggered at Saint-Merri; the door stays half-open on the stairhead: Who could walk in? A client who got the time wrong? A police officer? A pimp? It's snowing; the skylight shines with a faint blue light; the sparrow, feathers puffed, shifts place on its rags; at the skylight, a black shadow: a crow who peck-drinks the snow? Did they go out to replenish our supplies, theirs and mine? Will I have to eat? Break the fast of my anguish? From the stairhead comes a strong odor of boiled fish: a door has opened there; an old woman with gray hair, black dress with white polka dots, holds in her hands a steaming earthenware dish against her ample breast; a black cat follows her, between her legs, paws high, tail raised; the sparrow flits about in the box; I turn onto my left side, reach out my arm, take the bird, slip it under the coverlet; the old woman pushes the door to with her foot, steps forward, sets the dish down on the oilcloth, takes hold of the cat, clasps it squirming against her chest, goes out; the sparrow sets itself at ease on my chest in the opening of my pajama jacket.

From far below in the staircase, a few piano notes in which I recognize a piece of music from the time when I was alive; the sparrow has come up onto my face, pecks at my lips, the remnants of sugared coffee.

The eel stew is partly devoured before the stroke of one; slices of eel slip down our esophaguses, the wine broth warms our cheeks; the sparrow staggers from plate to plate; the back of the black cat arches and bristles at the half-open door; standing at the edge of the bed, the girl, bare-chested, tries on bras, white, red, black; the brother, face radiant, nudges me with his elbow; a crucifix shines above the bed, with a sprig of boxtree wedged between the cross and the tortured body.

At dawn, when the girl returns from the streets, snow on fur, smeared makeup, flesh smelling of spilled seed, the brother gets out of bed, slips in beside me again, beneath the coverlet; washed, she turns out the light, goes to bed, falls asleep with whistling, plaintive snores.

Two days. Dressed again, I write down their intertwined lives in a little new notebook; I read them the sentences in which I have adapted their phrases, rejoinders, exclamations; they want adjectives; I don't want any: nothing but facts, the smallest ones. We agree to a few adjectives. I also write their separate thoughts for each of them in a little notebook; she smiles at her brother's: the high seas, obedience, loyalty; he is shocked at his sister's: disillusioned, raw.

The leftovers of eel stew sustain us, with pasta or rice.

One day at noon—with the texts completed the night before; she having bathed standing upright in the tub, put on makeup, perfume—we go up on foot to Pigalle; her bag stuffed with flounces and feathers, she wants to get hired at the Les Pierrots strip club: we leave her, in white fur, high heels on red-brown snow, at the club's dark door. The brother takes my shoulder; his entire body is shaking, both from the cold wind flowing toward Montmartre and from the thrusts that his half sister's body is now suffering in the velvet half-light. Reopen my heart—intentionally shut—to their sorrow? Risk bringing myself back to life?

Let my being do as it will, alone; when pressed it will lead me to what it wants: its extinction; cast out from all others, living or dead.

As what's left of my heart grows weak at the sight of their anguish, and the anguish of those we see in the doorways laying out their cardboard shelters beneath the falling snow, my resolve to run away, to escape their candid tenderness, grows stronger; my being demands it.

Shake off this rough palm from my shoulder, hop onto the first city bus: the bus drives down the somber Rue de Clichy through the snow to La Trinité. I walk back along the Left Bank to my lodging house, get into bed there, warm myself, sweat out my fever until morning.

The hotelkeeper, as I pass the reception desk, reproaches me for not having informed her of my absence—my band of friends has come round each day—she gives me some mail, a letter from my father with the address written by one of my sisters. His handwriting, hasty, urgent, electric, is decipherable to me only if I imagine him thinking out the letter and shaping the characters of his wrath; I have to bring the letter to an ancient church to read it before the altar and its lit tabernacle.

    I go to open the letter and look at it in Saint-Julien-le Pauvre, where my mother, when she was in Paris, would come to pray before the iconostasis, an image, albeit under papal authority here, of the Russia that was close to her heart as a child and that would remain so in France when she was a young girl and then a married woman—she who had been born French in Poland, near Krakow. But sitting out of sight of the gold-clad officiants now withdrawing, I push away her memory and that of Flaubert's Saint Julien; I open the envelope, unfold the letter, fix my gaze on the sight of the red-lit Holy Sacrament, touch the letter; the freshly traced characters should yield their sense to me at the touch of my fingers. The little red light flickers, dims; the lights on the pillars go out: a power outage, too much snow?

I go out, cross the Seine, the letter in my inside pocket against my chest; I walk north, by way of the east—Père Lachaise, Buttes Chaumont—past the swing bridge on Rue de Crimée, the frozen canals. On Chemin de l'Échange, between Aubervilliers and Saint-Denis, I enter a café, its low yellow ceiling dark with coal soot. "Arabic" music plays in the half-light, a small flute, darabukka, rustic viol; a girl comes and goes from the semidarkness, loins glittering to the thrusts of her dance; ornaments jingle on her chest which sheds clothes at each turn: banknotes, little wads of bills flutter around her; threadbare turbans, white, gold, vestments of the enemy at the time; from outside, the sound of boat horns, splintering ice, wind. I sit at a table where children let sink their sleeping heads.

Will I be seized here, abducted, thrown with slit throat into the street or the canal, my being escaping through the gash? The thought that I might live until my compulsory enlistment next fall—and die over there at the hand of their brothers—that my "being" might still hold out for a winter a spring a summer, topples my forehead onto the table. They bring me a bowl of scorching-hot black coffee which they refuse to take payment for. The girl has seen the blazer under my coat; she comes over to me; with the few words of Arabic I learned last summer from a seamstress from Stains, I answer her words, which I can't understand. I see, above her sharply upturned lip, the shadow of that very fine down that moves me in girls and women; the outbursts of her delicate voice, slightly raspy, cause the artery on her neck to throb beneath the tender, perfumed skin; everything here smells sweet, good, the humans, the instruments. The children, cheeks on the table, mutter at nightmares: over there, in Algeria, people are hunting humans down, killing; others will soon do the same. Night arrives at the café's glass door, beaten by the snow.

Shadows press against the glass, sounds of boots; the door opens, forced: police officers, unhelmeted but with batons in hand, burst in: I see a mimeographed sheet of paper pass from hand to hand to the dancer who stuffs it into her glittering corselet; we are pushed, lined up against both walls, the children guarded at the table by a police officer who keeps them there with his gloved hands at their shoulders; each man is searched, prodded, turban undone; I keep my hands up; a policeman turns to me, his helmet knocking against my waist, and asks me if I am one of them; I blurt out that I'm not worthy to be. Immediately—as he mutters that he can't see why, and within myself I know it's because my theft has made me unworthy of taking part in their righteous cause—my heart grows heavy, with the coffee they gave me still warm in my intestines, at the thought of Christ's betrayal by his bedrock apostle Peter, my namesake; the dancer has taken the two children onto her knees; her chest pulses: Will a corner of the mimeographed paper come from her corselet, whose red border moves with each of her replies to the interrogation? The police officer takes me by the shoulder again, pushes me toward the door, opens it, pushes me gently out. The pane of glass, fogged by the breaths of the interrogation, lights up with outbreaks of struggle. At the end of the cobblestoned alley between the low hovels that resound with infants' cries, the black waters of the canal give way to a long barge loaded with pale sand lit by little lamps, its sides ferrying the now refreezing ice.

I hide behind a worksite fence and wait for the door to open again: a big tawny mud-spattered cat stretches itself along my legs, mews; men come out, hands crossed behind their heads, pushed toward a blue van parked at the top of the icy cobblestone slope with its headlights dimmed; the men walk up to it, unturbaned, slipping; along and behind them are the police officers, helmets on again, batons upraised. With the men loaded up, the van starts off, spins its wheels on the ice, climbs the slope, disappears in its smoke. Go back to the café whose window has gone dark? Did the piece of paper remain between the dancer's breasts? Have the children been put to bed? From the base of the hovels, bodies come out, lanterns at their sides; the cat hisses and spits between my ankles: a rat? What bird, in this darkness where an owl wouldn't dare take flight? A viol squeaks; a light switches on upstairs. Could the dancer have been a boy stuffed with breasts, made up? Wasn't that him I saw in the group, hands at his skull, treading the snow between the police officers?

I return to Paris on foot, fall asleep quickly; in the middle of the night, I get up, go to the table under the mansard eaves, open the manuscript which is covered in dust: A pigeon stirs on the window pane—let it inside?

I unfold the letter again, hide the end under my palm, observe that there are more question marks than exclamation marks, that a few words, which I decide to decipher later, have been crossed out— too violent or too emotional?—I go back to bed.

The next morning, the snow in the eaves thaws around the dead pigeon with its legs in the air; I breathe in the sunlit air; far off to the north, on the other side of the river, is the Marais and its threads of smoke—distilleries, little factories topped by unsteady chimneys, coal furnaces; on the downstairs landing, the ice melts between the footrests of the pan of the Turkish toilet; having eaten bread, oil, salt, I go down toward the Seine with its foghorns and shattered drifts of ice; who or what gave me such a hard conscience, harder than original sin? Walking along the river all the way to Sèvres, I feel my conscience pricking at my chest, rattling about like a piece of fossilized matter. Crossing over near the bottom of Meudon to get away from the rich places I dread, I walk on between the town's two hills. I catch a scent of meadows and cow dung: a little blond girl jingles her empty milk can in her hand before the small muddy entrance to a low farmhouse where I hear cows mooing; she watches me watching her; in the streetcar, the jolts trouble and blot out her golden eyes, where I wanted to assure myself of this pensive little girl's trust.

One evening, I enter a barely heated movie theater to see Jean Renoir's *The Golden Coach* again; the letter from my father is in the inside pocket of my blazer: waiting for the film, among the motions of the others toward the caramel vendor who passes, the basket at her breasts, surrounded by the audience in overcoats, kindly faces, I take out the letter from the warmth of my chest and, removing my glasses, with my eyebrows against the paper, I read the end, the signature, not "your father" but "Papa"; the snow melts under my soles, not from the air's scant warmth, but as if from the warmth that runs down from my heart; the further the film advances, the more my heart tightens at the sight of these warm lives, presumed reality confounded with presumed theater, the sight of these interdependent communities, these gifts, revocations, these motley bodies seeking, mirroring, desiring each other; all of humanity, active here, false and true, from which I am excluded; these colors redoubling their vitality that tears me apart; this golden coach, heavy and hollow, the anguish of its emptiness seizes me like that of my own within my earthly envelope; I go out with the others, my eyelids gathering my tears.

That night I awake from a dream in which my family duplicate themselves on stage, fall over themselves laughing at the looks on their faces in real life: What if I began to see beyond the theft, beyond the scene of the interrogation, or at least through the half-open door to the living room where I stand tortured? And what if, taking up with a troupe of traveling players, I acted out my misfortune, separation, madness, until I finally warded them off? And, by acting, began to master the scene of the theft, returned to my eagerness back then to stage the dispersal of my family so I could accomplish it in peace, and then, once the theft is discovered, go rigid—to have a laugh, to get a laugh—at my refusal to confess? But my conscience refuses to place, to move my father about in this play, this party of laughter. I fall back asleep.

The next day, helped by my brisk pace, walking southward, as I pass a number of fathers of all kinds surrounded by their children and adolescents playing, as I mimic their commands, their familial expressions, in a play of expressions I draw nearer to him again until I can smell the odor of tobacco and ether on his jacket, feel it brush against me: and then, in deepest secrecy, away from the too-close presences that might see into my mind, and with my eye fixed upon almost nothing, a flow of oil on the concrete, I dare to imagine him as a marionette moved by something larger than all of us that snatched away our mother, his fiancée, his wife, the mother of his six children, his soul, our soul; a puppet forced to make an accusation against me when I have come from his seed; at the intersection of three streets, I have a brief vision of me as a child sleepwalking, of him coming out one winter night from the marriage bed, bare feet on the tiles of the entrance, in a pale nightshirt, to stir the white-hot coals in the boiler, and a musty reek of sperm rises to my nostrils; is our mother asleep? Awake? But my conscience rejects seed and pantomime, organic origin and common wisdom: my conscience, through my small acts of painting and later of poetry, is moral law fortified by beauty; the Gospel fortified by the Old Testament; Christ's forgiveness does not take humanity as figures on a stage, easily absolved, irresponsible, nor life as a moveable theater.

But my theft is beyond these two authorities: God himself, the Creator, cannot unbind me from this theft, tighten the cord of my life again, and so I experience the isolation that, as a child, I attributed to objects, to small, apparently hostile animals, the crab before I saw it move its eyes; did He forget to create me? And am I human? Merely as species; and I suffer only because of the importance placed by religion and anti-religion on the human condition.

But how can I get out, alive, from the condition of being human, get out of so-called human being and remain alive?

The multitude of all that touches my foot, my eye, my ear, my sense of smell, and to which I must attribute a state, brief or a thousand years old and more, quickens my pace and the beating of my heart; I am out of Paris; in the Parc de Sceaux, before nightfall, in front of the Petit Château's stone grotto, a touchable image of the mixing of kingdoms, of the abstraction through which I must pass for Being to resume its place in me.

A few days later, my brother, eight years older than I, back from Algeria where his military service kept him for thirty-two months, comes to see me: for the first time in nearly two months I can embrace and allow myself to be embraced. That he knows so little about the nocturnal drama of the theft shows me that the act is on its way to being forgotten by the protagonists of what I experienced as a drama; and all while leaving me no doubt that he can see its effect on me— my hollow features, tremors, my violent appetite in which he recognizes his own not so very long ago when, during the Occupation, in his secondary school relocated under the bombardments to the Forez plain, he was cold and hungry under his schoolchild cape—he soothes me, his hand on mine as it slices and sauces, but my throat still refuses. And with the distance he gained in Algeria from this dramatization that he rejects, and with his experience as the firstborn child on whom our parents cut their teeth, and as a conscious witness to their anguish at the imminent war, to their sorrow at the defeat, then to their tension as some of their brothers and sisters joined the Resistance and were arrested and deported, and to my father's worry for his patients amid the shortages of food, medicine, and transportation, my brother disapproves of this mimicry of a verdict that has put me into the state he sees me in, and he laughs at me affectionately for having ever believed in it; I feel a shiver of blood pass through my veins: resist the languor of having a lineage. I come from nothing except myself who begins at this moment, and the being that lay heavy upon me on Earth is shattered.

At the Louvre, in front of Titian's *The Entombment of Christ*—which he and I, younger, our mother still alive, had once admired in a monograph he brought back from a stay, in Hamburg under reconstruction, with a family that had resisted Hitler; but to see that Germans, after having criminalized the world and defiled humanity, could continue to produce beauty and the critique of beauty had troubled us—with brief tears on his shoulder, I give in, just to keep on living; I am that body they carry to its tomb: but only to rise again, greater still, face washed of all illusions.

Slaughter my I, live without. Without restraint, the senses alone, animal. Exist without being.

Prisons

MY HAND clenches itself on the rail of the staircase descending from the dormitories, to make certain I truly exist; I have decided to cry out to all my fellow conscripts that they must awake from this bad dream: our enlistment, our drills—for hours on end, decompose the *present arms* into several motions, march past, perfect the *at attention*, the salute (in dance, such rigor gives rise to spectacle, to beauty), begin to handle arms, take aim at silhouettes, kneel down, touch the bazooka that knocks us on our backs, throw offensive grenades, defensive grenades (more dangerous), complete the obstacle course, close combat, and then the Corps of Engineers exercises: mine laying, mine detection, bridge construction... our submission, the ignorance in which we are kept about what is and what's to come, are a nightmare from which—break the spell of stupidity—we must wake in laughter; I do it, cry out exhortations, call people by name, point my finger at them, face-to-face with those who, for seven days already, have forced us into submission; I cry out that we must turn everything into farce; I appeal to a few of my fellow conscripts whom I know to be in agreement with my rebellion, but I am already strapped up, pinned against the handrail, then, struggling, against the stone steps; I pretend to relax, slump down, surrender; their grip loosens; I heave myself back up, shove about, run down the rest of the steps, lunge at the—hastily locked—door to the company commander's office, smash it in, burst into the double room where the stove roars, sweep the folders off the tables with both hands, come out again and drag down a set of shelves, hit objects and inkwells and equipment with a piece of firewood; unhook the uniform jackets from the coatracks, tear the stripes and medals off them with my hands and teeth, begin to beat the windowpanes, the stove, set open its loading ports. The recruits who serve as secretaries shield themselves with their arms, but I would not hit those who might follow me in this farce; the stove knocked over, the parquet floor strewn with debris among the spilled violet ink, I spring toward the captain's office, barehanded, rush at him as he rises to his feet behind two officers who have me seized by soldiers—our elders, obedient conscripts or regular army brutes?—and strapped down again; carried away to the infirmary— me biting at their arms, hands, faces, kicking at their legs—by way of the courtyards where I try once more to escape; I hear my fellow conscripts shouting, applauding, from our building all the way to the infirmary, from the upper-story windows, the ground-floor windows, the training grounds.

But as soon as the door shuts upon a half-darkness that tastes of ether, I hear nothing but the yelling of an officer, short, round, well fed, perfumed, whom everyone—medical orderlies, able-bodied patients—presses around, solicitous.

His large flabby hand tries to make me bend my neck as I am pushed onto a tall stretcher, immobilized on the taut cloth, strapped down by my ankles, knees, belly, forearms, throat; the officer, whose shoulder stripes I have time to see—chief warrant officer, gold with red trim—undoes the belt from his waist, brandishes it, coiled like a whip, and flogs my entire body; the leather—or the buckle?—flays my upper lip; do I still have my glasses or did they take them off me before the blows, for fear that the army would have to pay the cost of them?

Is it from a blow to the eyes or from my bare vision that I can see nothing but black, only the band of leather beneath a faint circular glow ebbing from the ceiling and around me whom the blows do not cause to cry out? The officer withdraws; his aides strike me with their belts; my eyelid bleeds; blood runs from my split lip; I want to drink it but as I stick out my tongue the strap chokes me: they loosen it for me.

In the evening, the officer and his aides return from the mess with scraps that they eat at a table, close to the stretcher where I stay on the alert; their jaws noisy on purpose, they take turns standing up and examining my trembling, which is calmer now, and one of them, the one who hit me most violently, takes my pulse; I keep my jaws shut so tight I could break my teeth; but during the beating some of the straps came loose, and when the chief warrant officer comes near, eating a scrap of chicken, I sit up, spit in his face with the blood of my mouth, and as he lowers his head toward me, I seize one of his shoulders, throw him backward, topple him onto his aides who have run to his side. Silence, fumblings at the far end of the half-light; straps readjusted; I feel someone take my arm, a finger searches for a vein on my wrist, a syringe plunges into it; I go entirely slack; my head rolls to the side; the froth dries around my lips; I want to continue the useless combat, but no nerve, no muscle responds anymore; what is it about me, about my form, that causes them to fear I could still resist, so that one of them cracks his belt again? I try to raise my chest, then my back, and then to raise myself on my elbows, in vain; could I have been given a lethal dose? Sweat fills my eyes; my wounded eyelid has swelled; I can no longer feel my ankles; will I meet my end on this stretcher, between these closed walls, with the assistants arranging my fingers and the straps for me to appear as if I strangled myself? And if I can no longer feel my arms, my hands, my fingers, it means they have committed a murder, they have murdered me: and, the deed done, they've vanished, like the murderers in *Macbeth*, from which I have taken the name of Donalbain, one of the children of Duncan the assassinated king, as a pseudonym for the text whose publishing contract I received yesterday, my father having refused that I sign it with his patronym; can I even, still two years away from legal adulthood, sign the duplicate sheets of the contract that I keep in my barrack-room locker?

Straps fall from my limbs, I feel them slip from my arms, my legs, with their buckles, like snakes from an ancient body, an allegory; a light moves about in the half-darkness.

The beam approaches, sweeps over my face; I feel myself taken by my arms, my back, my legs, lifted, carried toward a lit corridor and then outdoors, night—is it evening? Is it the morning of a following day? My porters cross one courtyard, then two, my glasses—lenses broken? cracked?—are in a pocket of my drill uniform jacket. Before us is the broad vestibule of the barracks above which I see, with my vague eyesight, backward and superimposed upon the regiment's numbers and letters, the motto of a Nazi camp or the command at the entrance of the third canto of Dante's *Inferno*. And yet, since childhood, I have withstood every roll call in the cold at boarding school, every wait at a ticket window or elsewhere, by comparing them to those the deportees were subjected to in the camps. The transport vehicle parks in front of a low building connected to the gatehouse; clanks of heavy keys, locks, door bolts; they take me into the darkness, roll me onto a strap bed; the darkness smells of winter water, sweating stone, a wet blanket, and human excrement; the door closes again, locks; a shape moves near the back wall; I pull my glasses out of my pocket; the brief movement pains my entire body from skull to toes; my heart beats harder from it: I exist, earthly; I have not passed the threshold of the hereafter toward which I felt myself tugged to be hurled into it.

The bugle plays reveille, its stupid motif. So it's predawn. The shape, as it moves again, gives off a fresh odor of defecation; wait for morning, a light—filtering from where?—to see the odor's body. How, sore down to my littlest joints, can I roll out of this straw mattress that teems with vermin beneath me, beneath the damp fabric—soiled?—of my clothes torn by the blows?

I fall asleep; when I wake up, a light under the door; at the back, the shape turns over on the straw mattress of a strap bed; a sound of jawbones, a moan; the door, unlocked, opens upon a soldier carrying a little pot of hot coffee, steaming; the light shows me the shape's body, prone, its fist between its bloodied jaws; fatigues soiled below the waist; a pile of excrement has been pushed from the back of the cell under the bed; the soldier sets down the pot, supports me as I try to sit up on the mattress; from the misty outdoors, a large, flabby voice shouts out an unidentifiable word; the soldier pulls away his hand, his arm from beneath my back, returns to the pot, plunges the ladle into it, fills two dented mugs, sets them on the black dirt floor, goes out, leaves open the crude door, worm-eaten at the bottom; I see white worms move on the black feces; the same kind as the ones on the walls of shitters overflowing with the Monday-morning vomit of the soldiers back from leave that, for two weeks, I have been spraying with cresyl: cleaning shitters exempts one from the exercises of submission, isolates from the shouts, the repeated commands: retreat into waste as a retreat into nature.

My gaze, beneath my injured eyelid, rises higher: jaws knock at the tin mug, pale eyes behind the steam; the whole body trembles, the half-bared shoulders, the teeth, very white at the front, sharp-pointed at the corners, leave the mug; fleshy lips, their line visible beneath the drying blood, wrinkles rolling on the short luminous forehead beneath short, bloody black curls: the nose broken.

Could it be the fellow conscript, unseen, of Italian ancestry on his father's side, Gypsy on his mother's side, the apprentice steel-frame worker, nearly professional boxer, whose suicide attempts are gossiped about throughout the barracks?

Drawn to the warmth or the opening to outside, a rat leaps from the semidarkness beyond the excrement, scurries between the combat boots of the soldier returning with his pot; the conscript, from the back, where he holds out his mug again, whistles a motif, soft, between his teeth and reddened lips, the tip of his tongue appearing between his front teeth to form a hissing sound that makes the rat stop in its tracks and turn around on the icy slab.

 The soldier goes back out to the entrance pavilion, the door closes again, the rat slips back into a corner hole beneath the bed-planks. The conscript, one wrist bandaged, the other bloodied, explains to me that he owes this rat charm to his childhood in a hovel in Vienne above the Gervonde, from which buck-rats and she-rats and rat pups would on stormy nights come up between the slats of the floor above which swung the last-born's cradle; his mother then would hum a motif she learned from her own mother as she drove the rats away from the basket spilling into the mud with the baby among the storm flows, in camps on the outskirts of the cities of Eastern Europe. I gaze at his bare wrist, the torn flesh, bitten with his own teeth along the veins; they say that, escaping from the chief warrant officer and his henchmen, traitors to their own kind as conscripts, he climbed along the gutter of a barracks rooftop to slash his wrists again on the razor wire there. To the regimental authorities, this "volunteer," recruited in exchange for the remission of a prison sentence for attempted armed robbery, is a "wound" to their honor; to us, to me, waking from combat, he is a tortured prisoner who has rid himself, is ridding himself, of his bonds, of the instruments of his torture, again and again, another cut in an unfinished wound; a ray of sunlight filtering through the dirty, cracked pane of a small window below the sweating ceiling illumines his irradiant face, his injured ears, the rasp of his voice in which I can hear, by the sounds that come as if through broken teeth, from within his infected intestines and his puffing-unpuffing cheeks, that he has decided to die, trapped on all sides—by his origin, the law courts, his recruitment—and that only boxing and at-height work have delivered him for a time from the death that envelops him in its black halo.

 The remains of a fire smolder in the farthest corner of the building, named "Marengo"; the ray of light, as it declines—already, before noon?—lights up some graffiti on the wall where our bed-planks are fastened: hearts, ball sacks, cunts, cocks, arrows planted in hairy orifices, a few inscriptions—"Death to the Brass," "Death to the Army"—a woman worked from the front by a dog, heads effaced; I see him look and lower his eyelids, the tops of his cheeks blushing beneath the crusts under his slightly slanted eyes; the smallest of his movements, even a smile, sends forth an odor of excrement, but sweet, touching, like that of a baby in swaddling clothes: each time, he looks around, as if the smell, of which he knows he is the source, came from someone else; every time we move, the rat runs beneath the bed-planks. Is this the only vaulted ceiling in the building? Stand up from the bed-planks again, step forward, grope about in the dark, reach another vault, touch other inscriptions, etched, from the previous century, Communards, convicts of the December 2 coup?

In the evening, two plates of beans later, scrape up the pile of feces with a shovel, throw it into the pit, wash the leavings, the remnant, with cresyl; in the guardroom roars the stove which they force me, the potential arsonist, to refill with fuel; epaulettes glitter their gold through the smoke as the booted officers come and go; through the cell's half-open door I see him, beltless, laces removed from his combat boots, like me; he stands trembling, mug in hand, his three-day-old excrement gluing his fatigues to his bottom, to his legs, his liquid eyes filled with tears; the water in the pot is still steaming; they throw me a sponge, a brush; I have him undress from the waist down, take off his socks, combat boots; with his feet in the cresyl sudsing on the dirt floor, his wounded fists clenched before his parts, a gash of red across the dark sky, the clatter of the trains beyond the street, the close river smashing its frozen mud, I no longer feel my wounds and bruises; I am seized with rage again, that instead of forcing me to decompose my motions into three parts, to shove my cheek and shoulder against the murderous rifle, they don't assign me to this, which suits me, to nursing, consoling, restoring courage; I take him by the shoulder, bring him to the pot in the small courtyard covered with a cracked glass roof, dip the sponge in the hot water, scrub him, turn him round, soap his bottom, the bend of his knees, his feet, pour water all over his lower body, without touching his front parts, which I have him soak and wash with soap, and with what grace he cleans each fold of them, each tuft; the quartermaster sergeant, who comes from my region and who raised his fists at the aides when he saw them continue to strike me this morning as they shoved me toward the cell, brings us a pair of fatigues riddled with holes, too short but clean; the soiled fatigues are tossed in the trash; a cloth falls on my shoulder from behind; I rub the conscript's entire lower body with it; I feel the muscles relax, his weight, light, fresh, teeters back and forth, topples onto me; the body is laid on the bed-planks again, its face pale, a little blood appearing on the purplish lips; with help I slip him into fatigues that reek of gas and leather: From what body have they assumed these forms, on the far shore of the Mediterranean, perished, putrid, castrated?

After lights-out, I am brought back to the infirmary; the chief warrant officer, in acknowledgment of my tenacity, has me eat at his table: a rumor is running through the barracks that I stood up to him; I have learned from one of his aides, who has begun to betray him, that he holds a sham diploma as a pharmaceutical assistant and traffics with other local pharmacists in the medicine and high-cost materials allotted to the regiment, and so I am not surprised to hear him offer me his friendship and assure me he will protect me from now on. What does he want from me? That I become his accomplice? Could my late-December theft be known to the military police? That this thief who confers such equivocal accolades would count me as one of his own throws me into an inward rage again, but for the sake of getting my cellmate better food, medical care, and a hospital room— from which he could escape and get to Switzerland—I give him my best smile; until lights-out I walk the length of the largest courtyard speaking of politics and art with the little second lieutenant of my platoon who has come to fetch me from the infirmary; he tells me that when they emptied out and inspected my barracks-room locker, they found a long letter from a girl, written in very round blue characters, treating of love and not-love; and so the chain of command has judged my crisis to be due to a broken-off flirtation. For me, to have received this letter informing me of the cessation of desire in her—Sophie—for me on the same day that I received my first publishing contract makes me laugh and tremble: love is forbidden me so that I create.

As winter advances, our Corps of Engineers exercises—bridge assembly and installation on the Isère River—take place between the ice floes; one noonday, between the nine-o'clock bread-break and lunch on the riverbank, as our own barges drift on the frothy current and another company's barges struggle to assemble the metal beams, I recognize my prison mate in the maneuver; he stands, his back arched, eyes uneasy, his mouth smeared with the same pale-red pâté as ours, with one foot on a riser, the other on the barge; he finishes locking into place a piece bigger than himself; as a mass of ice shatters against the barge, his foot gives way; my prison mate falls between the barge and the riser, onto a sheet of ice where the sun at its zenith shines pale red through the floe; he holds himself there with his elbows; I see the whites of his eyes sparkle amid the pale red, seeing me; does he want to let himself drown without a cry, or does he want to be saved, sent to Algeria to let himself be killed there as an enlisted man on the front lines? His army mates reach out a pole to him, an oar... he grasps it, hoists himself out of the icy water, shakes off the water thick with mud; his wrist, which he was trying tear to pieces with his teeth in prison, is bandaged, same as the other one...

... At the center of the barracks' main courtyard, among the still fragrant traces of the heaps of autumn leaves gathered by hand, our company stands at attention; upon orders, a few of us step out from the row: those with exemptions as sole family providers; candidates for officer reserve training, which defers deployment to Algeria—a track my IQ test marked me out for but that I refused, both out of fear of being subjected to unpleasant gymnastic and mathematical exercises, and out of a desire to test myself, at the very bottom of the chain of command, in a war that, at the time, was becoming complicated as new factions emerged; to put a sea between an uncertain "I" and the remnants of paternal authority and their extension in the hierarchical strictures of the mainland barracks.

We are to leave tomorrow. The colonel, in parade dress, gold braids, medals glinting in the winter sun, takes a leaflet from his breast pocket and reads it to us in a firm voice: I hear him say that we are setting out to defend civilization from communism; the dead leaf that clings to his combat boot is stronger than this leaflet's succession of very rapidly pronounced words—having left our minds with our civilian clothes, there is no need, as he sees it, for us to concern ourselves with reasons.

Before the "Vive la France," I make out the word "ambassadors": we all look at each other, straight-backed but tattered, our Alpine Corps of Engineers "*tarte*" berets clapped onto our resprouting hair; brought to submission, humiliated, shouted at from all sides, our language depleted, our spirit negated, we will be the ambassadors of France and Western civilization ... Quick! To the trucks, the train, the boats!

Worksites

THE GIRL, a half-wit, runs across the dried clay roofs of the huts; soldiers from a nearby company that has rights to the douar run after her, her chest bare, her shoulders exposed beneath a gold-and-red scarf; I see them through my glasses, obscured with dust and flecks of cement, among the Barbary figs flowering again beneath the remains of the snow; we haul stones on trucks from a quarry up above, riding on the footrests down to our worksite: a winding road from the plain to the interior of the Ali Bounab Massif; we unload the stones there with bare hands; split, cut; we set the even-shaped pieces in the roadbed; a machine levels them; once the road is paved, we build the shoulders, the gutters, the bus lanes, the small bridges; each of us signs his name, the date, in the fresh concrete, the work made by his hand alone: I write mine on the edge of a gutter that the hooves of donkeys will tread upon this summer.

We sleep under large tents that we pitched as soon as we arrived at the site down below, some distance from the douar patrolled by vigilante groups of armed farmers and shopkeepers; two, then three half-tracks stationed beside the roadbed protect us; machine-gun fire by day, by night—each time, we have to get out of our meatsacks dotted with the blood of bedbugs, rise from under the rough, dusty blankets, seize our weapons from the rack, retrieve our heavy helmets, light helmets—we work and live in light helmets—and wait on the perimeter of the camp, USM1 rifles in hand.

Three months of open air, pure night, my chest and arms strengthened, a discipline accepted, no shouts—everyone keeps quiet on this territory where everything is watched. Spring: the bees dance in the drafts of newly fragrant air; hares, at the sound of gunshots, scamper off above us; here and at home, in Cairo, in Switzerland, there are hints of negotiations; one night, when I step outside the tent to piss by the latrines, where some jackals that have come to rummage their muzzles through our excrement for something to eat scatter with a yelp, I hear, distant but clear in the radiance of the full moon that lights the summits and depths, from within the commotion of the douar, a strangled cry, like, not so long ago on the outskirts of pig or poultry farms, the cries drowned in the blood of a slit throat; a faint light skips between the huts: Are such deeds done even in broad moonlight, God the Creator lighting the crime of his creatures, when in thick night everything would be possible? The cry is not that of a grown man, not that of a grown voice that has already decided, ordered, calculated, covenanted, uttered love, taken the battle oath, but that of a fresh voice, from a tender neck where the vein blends in with the flesh.

Third part of April: the chain of command having transferred me for radio-operator training to an airport in Greater Kabylia where the small T6s and large Sikorskys take off and land, I learn Morse code. Its signals, rightly understood, recall the logic of sounds in music and poetry; our sergeant instructor, an academic who is already a scholar of occultism, illuminism, Rosicrucianism, and vampirism, finally finding someone to speak with, lets me practice, learn, as I please.

On our little Sonolor transistor whose connections I repair with a soldering iron, we hear a news report over a background of roaring crowds in Algiers: French generals have seized power there and mean to extend their coup to the mainland; on the national road—which passes from Tizi Ouzou to Azazga through the already sweltering basin, and then runs alongside our camp with departmental roads branching out on both sides—an unusual movement of jeeps, command cars, and GMCs puts us on the alert; as we begin to scatter outside the barbed wire, the camp commanders assemble us all in one of the large overheated hangars where, at the back, mechanics busy themselves with one of the machines that drop napalm on the forests, machine-gun the douars abandoned under duress; on a platform near the entrance, a few officers bustle about—low bows, salutes, snaps to attention—their berets and kepis in hand, swagger sticks tapping at their knees; they are from various divisions, air force, infantry, artillery, airborne; the rest of us, common soldiers, privates, lance corporals, corporals, reserve sergeants, stand pressed against each other in a mass facing them, all of us from district regiments; we swap information, rumors, fragments of speeches from the generals in Algiers, from General de Gaulle in Paris, signs of our approaching deliverance or of an anarchy we might profit from; in the haste of our exchanges, words from our civilian speech return to us, with throaty laughter that we will have need of in answer to the arrogance of the officers now calling out for silence; according to the highest-ranking of them, this is all just a generals' quarrel (General Challe victorious; de Gaulle jealous): it is incumbent upon the troops to follow their field commanders; the most senior soldiers among us, deferred conscripts, wise, having already cast their votes in elections, begin to protest with raised hands; we raise our own hands, seconded by our voices, some only recently freed from an adolescent cracking; we assert the authority of right over might, of the elected president over the factious generals who have no mandate; news runs through the ranks that General de Gaulle, constitutional commander of the armed forces, has demanded of us, the conscripts (illegally coerced to wage war), that we cease to obey those who have ceased to obey him, ceased to obey the Republic; in life, this notion of right vs. might that we all intoned without conviction in class as we sat at our textbooks opened to a different page, or to a postcard pinup, now fills our hearts like the flush of blood in a teenager's cheeks; and we stand elbow to elbow and all but sway to the rhythm of the discovery. Some soldiers who came to support their factious officers leave the hangar; the platform empties out; one of us climbs onto it and sits there, cross-legged, the guitar that he went out to fetch from his locker resting in the crook of his thigh; he plucks the heat-slackened strings; outside, at the camp gate, from trucks loaded with paratroopers, voices call out for us to join them; the most senior soldiers organize a night watch; the last of the officers from the other regiments leave the camp in jeeps; our own officers, who have heard their hesitant voices drowned out for an instant by our own, now grudgingly recall us to our duties and equipment: encryption; P3; P6; walkie-talkies; battery-powered field phones; "*gégène*" generators with their straddle cranks; battery-powered vehicular appliances; antennae.

The entire night, we take shifts at the camp entrance, for fear that, as long as the generals in Algiers haven't fled or surrendered, the factious soldiers might come back to surround us and force us to join them; there is talk of officers captured by their men and shorn.

At the end of the training course, in the middle of a scorching-hot summer, our sergeant instructor raises my grades to the point that I obtain a chief-radio-operator certificate; in the meantime, I have received the package with the copies of my first little published book that my father sent on to me, torn and accompanied by another letter of admonishment, which I go off on my own to read, splashed by the water spurts the army mates spray at each other from dawn to midnight, when we fall fitfully asleep on the drenched straw mattresses of our metal bunks.

She walks through the snow; what does she have on her feet, knotted rags? A long khaki overcoat conceals her bare shoulders and upper chest, her slender haunches molded by a blue-and-gold dress; a scarf of the same color binds her auburn hair: the shadowy complexion of her face, which holds the hint of a withdrawn smile as she passes between the outpost's seeping drystone wall and me looking for the right place to put my antenna, is the same gently worried complexion as that of my mother at the age of seventeen, after her own mother's death; from a nook in the snow-covered rampart walk where I drive my stakes, I see her shake the snow from her rag-covered feet on the stone slab outside the offices of the platoon that controls the outpost, enter the room where the stove glows red, take hold of a wicker broom, and, with a thrust of her hips, sweep the small dirt-floored room next to the space where I have installed my devices and their generator.

The outpost is built atop a crest at the edge of the last ravine before the Djurdjura Massif, face-to-face with its summit, Lalla Khedidja, snow-covered all year round; in between radio-transmission sessions, I join my army mates, who are clearing the road with shovels and pickaxes, exposed as soon as they have emerged from the narrow passes with cover from the clifftops and from the half-tracks that accompany their convoys front and back; my father having been slow to sign the necessary documents for the military administration, I wasn't able to return to the mainland to attend the ceremony of his remarriage—for which I sent him my blessing, the necessity of his earthly consolation taking precedence, temporarily, over the purity of the celestial bond from which we issued; is he, on this day, slipping another ring onto the finger of the young woman, lively of heart and mind, chosen by my sisters?

From the table where I clumsily send and receive the required messages, I hear the captain—who has come from the depth of the ravine, from his battalion—raise his voice in the neighboring office, separated from me by a plywood partition: a voice, gentle, willful, melodious, replies in Kabyle mixed with Army French; the male voice grows harsh, growls, bursts out; the melody echoes it, slips itself into the silences, twines round the heavy words; the broom scrapes against the dirt floor again; a fellow soldier, whom the medical orderly has absolved from outdoor duty, straddles the generator, spins the crank; I manipulate the controls; the loudspeaker before me sends back the replies, the commands from soldiers at headquarters whom I picture manipulating their controls amid beer cans, open pâté tins, pornographic "books"; the plywood door opens; the captain touches only the shaft of the broom; his other hand points to the generator and its revolving crank; the young woman draws back; her words rush from her mouth; the wind, outside, whips and lifts the snow in the darkness that rises from the ravine.

Sleeping on a cot beside my table, where the equipment crackles until midnight, I wake up, enter the empty office in the light of the moon: on the table is a copy of *The Iliad*, the same as mine not so long ago, the Leconte de Lisle translation, published by Alphonse Lemerre in Passage Choiseul, publisher and bookseller of the Parnassian and, later, the Symbolist poets whose pages I so often thumbed through as an early adolescent in the secondary-school library; did the captain, a young man whose strict uniform curbs a rebellious body, forget the book here, or did he leave it for me to find, and, along with it, a part of the secret that his light eyes dazzle us to hide?

I do not touch it, but it all comes back to me: Astyanax, Andromache, Hector, Patroclus, Achilles, Hecuba, Cassandra, the dung and blood in the Achaeans' nostrils after they have slit the throats of sheep and oxen, the sleep of the rage-filled Achilles, son of Peleus, in his tent, and Priam's sleep, outside, among the treasure that is to pay for

Hector's corpse, its face arranged for his father, to whom the Greeks have already sold seventeen sons.

Where does the young woman sleep? In her father's hut? In a sideshed attached to the captain's room in the depth of the ravine where the snow is now rehardening? The next morning, her scent, musk, precedes her entrance into the room where the stove roars again; the captain enters, glances at the book toward which the woman reaches her henna-rubbed hand; I set to work on the messages again: snow-removal status, ambush risk, supply deliveries, promotions; through the partition, I hear the dialogue begin again, weary threats, gentle protestations, interrupted by the scraping of the broom against the dirt floor, the dusting of the shelves, then, from an adjoining shed, the clattering of pots, plates: I can hear that subordinate officers are now filling the smoky space of the office with the rustling of their combat uniforms; that one of the young woman's brothers is in the Resistance and is suspected of controlling a douar with a small troop of fighters and of having slit the throat of a shopkeeper in T. who refused to pay the "revolution tax"; she has allegedly been seen carrying a pitcher on her head and a bundle on her back walking toward one of the mountain gorges; standing outside on the stone slab, which I can see through a little window, she denies the allegation with open hands, lays a finger across her throat to suggest its fragility; the captain pulls forward in his jeep, orders the young woman into it.

They return from the depths of the inland valley before nightfall; I see him helping her step out, buttoning the top of her overcoat around her neck; I see her, on a chair in the office, collapse her arms, the small of her back, her neck, but with her arms on her knees she lifts her eyes to him as he stands shuffling through papers at the table; from what place has he brought her back to these heights where the setting sun glows red on the snow? From those places of the plain, now under thick night, that are said to be dedicated to the torture of suspects and their suspected accomplices? What torments, threats, stretched limbs, electric shocks, have given her this curved posture, these parched lips, these clasping, reclasping hands that she covers with the cuffs of her hole-ridden coat? She, too, three summers ago, the same shadow upon her brow and cheeks, among the firs and pines of our garden, braced her whole body, racked with sickness, against the chaise longue's armrests and covered, re-covered, her wrists with the cuffs of the coat that kept her warm in the August heat in which the birds above fell silent: the wren we never see, like the Phoenix that reengenders itself in solitude. Did he go down—he, the defender of Western civilization—to deliver her up to the civilian branch of the Division Opérationnelle de Protection? Late at night, when the young woman is in bed—lodged with a family in the douar?—he comes in to give me messages to transmit the following day, mine-clearing equipment requests—a sign of war's end—in his other hand he holds the book, shut: Does he know my thoughts, what some already accuse me of? Did he only bring her down to the DOP to deceive his commanding officers? Did he bring her before the building of the torturers, make her sniff beneath the doors and gates the stale stench of electricity, blood, excrement?... Could it be that he has decided to leave the army once the war is finished, his duty done? Could it be that he was still nearly a child when he enlisted?... Under what compulsion? His hand trembles: Is the young widow's brother surrounded now, by another company, in that chaos of ice and rock?... Why does he leave the book with me for the night?... Bent over me as I transform his orders into sounds, long and short, which I could just as easily transcribe into farce, he takes my signal manual and follows with finger and ear what I type out for him with the remains of the generator's power. Nearly all the colors have vanished from the piedmont. Could he be the Astyanax to some Andromache, already perished in the arms of, under the weight of, what Pyrrhus? His hand trembles: more than a captain's should.

The next day at noon, a small van puffs between the snowdrifts: men in torn djellabas, mud-bespattered, jump from the cargo bed; soldiers push them toward a low building covered in snow to its roof; a body remains behind on the corrugated-iron cargo bed; the legs, whose feet are bare, hang bloodied over the rear license plates; the army mates, having come from their barrack rooms, sweaters on their chests—

civvies for some, knitted by their mothers, sisters, or "war godmothers"—slosh through the melted ice, crane their necks inside the small van, icy-roofed, which has returned from higher up the massif's initial slopes: a buzzing of flies grows louder at the back; a filthy pallor appears there in the half-light, a face whose head is raised against the back of the driver's seat: blood still runs from the corners of the lips onto the bottom of the unshaven cheeks; behind us, the door to the office opens upon the young woman prisoner, held at the shoulder by the pale-faced captain; a brief cry; another stifled; will she grow pale, lose consciousness, collapse on the stone slab like Andromache seeing Hector's corpse from her balcony and collapsing all at once?

Which of us runs to the barracks, comes out holding a pair of khaki socks that another of us takes from him and slips onto the frozen feet of the corpse where, at the touch of the sun, the flies advance from the back of the vehicle, from the face toward the genitals?

The next day, she carries a nursling against her breasts and rocks him back and forth as she turns, standing on the sparkling snow in a striped qashabiya hood: In what language is the infant's cry? What information can be extracted from his cry?

Algiers

I RAISE my finger; a large antique-crimson car slows, stops short in front of me; the train, behind me, starts off from the station: on it are my army mates, whom I plan to meet up with again in Algiers in three hours, as long as there are no attacks or ambushes; under my khaki jacket, I have on a green civilian sweater; my shoes are the ones for leave. The driver, a large, portly man in a narrow beret, opens the rear door for me; seated on the left, an old man with thin, white, longish hair offers me his hand with two rings on two fingers; a folder of papers lies open on his knees; I sit down beside him; the car starts off, gains speed, enters the first curves; the air is already filled with the scent of blossoms; sheets of snow shine up above; the sky is almost violet by force of blue. The lanyard at my shoulder flutters in the draft of air filled with the distant rumblings of T6s toward the ocean. In Algiers I am supposed to meet a brave and kind man whose publisher, the same as mine, has, from Paris, arranged for him to welcome me. And then, with three of my army mates, to make the most of a thirty-six-hour leave.

But here I am beside an old man who pulls two pewter cups and a flask of cognac out of a leather pouch that hangs from the back of the front seat before him; with the curves becoming sharper, and knowing I am sensitive to them, in my gladness at being on leave and joy at the approaching ceasefire, I give in and drink; on coming out of the curves, we have to stop along the banks of a little wadi so I can vomit there; I hide behind some high reeds, press my palms against a piece of mudguard attached to the remnants of a car hood on a chassis sticking out from the sand, and vomit: not only occupy this land that belongs to others, but add my vomit to it too... farther on, a girl crouching at a washboard stirs laundry, pink, yellow, in the water laden with scraps of thawed mud; her haunches are belted with gold; and what if a gust of wind catches my vomit and carries its musty reek to her nostrils, opened wide to the water whose surface is skimmed by the first of the birds: teals! I need to vomit again; the driver stands with his shadow at my back; a column of insects has concentrated itself upon a swelling in the sand: if a line, then it might be an arm; if a circle, then a heart or castrated parts.

I walk back up to the car; we drive more slowly. Before the coastal plain, we pass three checkpoints; I've learned from the forcedly cheerful old man that he is a lawyer, that he is on his way back from Tizi Ouzo, where he has pleaded the case of a father who murdered his dishonored daughter, that modern law takes customary law into account, but that he wasn't able to save his client from a sentence of life in prison; descended from a family that traces its origins back to before the French colonization, and even, according to his research, to before the Arab conquest, he fears no one and will remain here, whatever comes of the peace; his assassin, he says, will have quick work finding the vein in his throat—the vein of a pleader of desperate causes.

In Algiers, along the heights, we enter, through a kitchen where a rooster in a caba crows full-throated beneath the table on which it will be strangled and plucked, through corridors of antiquated objects where the briefcase and folder come to rest on a cracked marble console, a garden where a fountain murmurs in the night, its sputterings lit by the beam of a spotlight from the watchtower of a distant barracks; my nausea persists; they have me stretch out on a chaise longue, and a washcloth with warm scented water passes over me from the hand of a woman who shuffles her feet along the glazed tiles; I resist the pull of sleep by gazing at the image of the crouching girl in my immediate memory, her haunches, her belt, what I could glimpse of her nape, the curve of her cheek—and what if the other cheek was maimed? In one of those massacres where people kill with whatever comes to hand, hammers, mauls, stones, scissors? Each time I turn or tilt my head, I see palm trees, tufts of feathers, big half-closed flowers; there are gunshots in the lower city; from a transistor radio on a round table, I hear that a group was machine-gunned the night before; listed in the bulletin, among the dead, is the man I am supposed to meet tomorrow.

Who is it that, at my instructions, tells my army mates I will spend the night here and meet back up with them tomorrow morning at the little seaside hotel that has a special rate for us?

For dinner, we do not eat the rooster but rather a quarter of wild boar whose flesh, though gamier and not as bitter, reminds me of the flesh of stray cats that our mess-hall chefs stir into their beef ragouts by way of supplement. The woman shuffles around the table in her babouches; her haunches smell very strongly, gnats flit in the light of her bosom.

The old man pushes me into his study, where a French door opens onto an alcove of the garden; I can only see what must be a third of the room, but almost everything I lack is here before me: music, by way of a piano and records; poetry, theater, prose, by way of books, translations from the Latin, Greek, English, and German, bilingual Old French editions; art books, reproductions, architectural drawings. Within three to seven minutes, I've recognized the bindings of works, collections, embraced with my eyes a portion of that which, for lack of means, has remained beyond my reach. An eye—dreamy from afar, filled with desire up close—belonging to one of Gauguin's Tahitian women juts from a pile in the half-darkness; Stravinsky's glasses, from a leaning stack of records; a thin booklet where my eyes, through lenses misted with fumes of wild boar, can make out Desnos's *Night of Loveless Nights*... from the far end of the study comes a sound of wing feathers scraping, opening, a pecking, a beak against the wires of a cage.

Where will I sleep? Can I sleep when there is so much here to read, look at, listen to? The old man's voice begins, frail, gentle, hardly dulled by the ingestion of savage flesh, in the half-light gilded by the glass lampshade; around midnight, the wind sways the palms outside; at any moment, the door could open upon murderers armed with knives or rifles; he, elbows at his table; I, before him, in the defendant's chair; until first light, name by name, work by work, period by period, I defend that which my body's, heart's, mind's youth, together with the practice of poetry, have caused me to hold as the beginning and end of all desire—the Luminaires of Time, the Lights of the West, certain immortality; all the things that he, the old man, has cast away, or casts away each day, since Earth and Time and Space are all as fragile as his own body, when the anguish seizes his knowledge, his consciousness, and hurls them into the infinite that cannot be thought; all emotions, artistic, social, amorous, religious, break themselves to pieces against it; old age and experience disintegrate the body no less than the atom does the world; how, as atoms, can we concentrate to think ourselves? Think, experience each of our atoms to think ourselves fixed, in sensations, words, themselves atoms? Think ourselves fragmented therefore, in a world that will perish, Earth, sun, stars, but then how think the perishing? Does every thought not lead to death, complete concentration to madness?

The greatest art—the immortality of which is all the more insisted upon for its being uncertain—hangs entirely upon a suspension of the urgent need to live, to survive, which creates reality and binds us to it; the greatest art hangs upon a lie, a veiling of the face...

I, for my part, have the future before me, which I have to fill with deeds, acts, new works; a body for doing.

Behind me, the sound of wings, beak, changes into muttering: A parrot? A mynah bird repeating the end of each desperate phrase, milling it in its beak with a little strident cry. The old man, each time, takes a flask and glass from out of the left-hand drawer of his desk, pours, drinks; I imagine a shiny pistol waiting in the right-hand drawer.

Long past midnight, he leads me—I imagine him in the previous century, a candlestick or oil lamp in his fingers—with his law-court hand, strong, resting on the finely worked banister decorated with marble, up to the third floor where, on a stairhead beside a window banging in the wind filled with all the scents of night, a bedroom lies open, prepared by the servant before she returned to her family in an upper shantytown: once he is back downstairs—from above, I watch, to be sure he makes it down without a fall, a feebleness of heart—I examine the place, its corners dusty, the paintings that tip forward from the walls covered in patterns of faded wallpaper; the sheets are turned down at the top: Will I dare to slip between them, my body battle-hardened but unbathed in seven days?

Under a large sink, whose tall curved faucet I do not turn on, I see cockroaches scurrying around the cracked drainpipe; but I do slip between the thick white sheets, so fresh, stretch my legs, my feet, all the way to the bars: try not to attract the cockroaches' attention—but what would they find on me to eat? From the open top drawer, I take out a Bible. I search for, find, reread Abraham's sacrifice: Does God demand of the human, as proof of his submission to Him, that he profane what is purest in this world: childhood, paternal love? That he profane the sacred in living flesh, as in the laboratories of Auschwitz... And the ram caught in the thicket, waiting to be slaughtered instead of the man-cub... Keep watch as long as I haven't heard him get into bed, on the ground floor, the creak of the mattress springs... I wake with a start, go down to see if the light still glows beneath the door to his study; a clacking comes from next to a neighboring house—a stork clacking its beak in dream?—and it becomes the pistol that he cocks... the mynah bird, in the back, toward the palms, still mutters in its slumber, the echoes of lost hope; back upstairs, between the sheets again, I reopen the Old Testament, find again, in words, in numbered verses, the images that our mother interpreted for us during the Occupation—us sitting on the little chairs brought home long ago from Upper Austria by our grandfather, her father—taking up the story of Moses again, begun the night before, the bush lit with fire two nights before, and still burning with fire and not consumed, the plagues of Egypt, of which we awaited the more familiar ones, the frogs, in summer, scarce, that croaked on the banks of the slightly stagnant river beneath the high wall of our apartment, the manna in the desert, more exquisite, in those times of hardship, than the few pastries and scattered sweets in the shopfronts; I slowly turn the pages, attentive to the sound of the swarming cockroaches; I go to Lot's wife, transformed into a pillar of salt as she looked back upon Sodom in flames—why not carry her along in the escape, on his shoulder, as a supply of salt?—like Orpheus looking back at Eurydice who vanishes at his gaze; on toward the patriarchs, those lively young men, tormented by spiritual desires yet unknown to me as a child; nobler, more heroic than the blood-soaked clowns in Homer and the Greek myths, with the exception of the daughters, Antigone, whose obstinacy in wanting to bury her brother I understand better here—how many like her!—as I see how corpses are violated, mutilated; on toward those old faces wrinkled with righteous unresolved enigmas, like the one posed by Goethe in his glory, devastated by an anguish that, as a lively adolescent, I could not understand: the enigma of death that makes you die for real, and its uncertain prolongation in the hereafter; the enigma of the gracious old man, my host, whose despair my youth at once suspends and magnifies.

The pages turn to Joseph, sold by his brothers, whom I have

recognized as a fellow across the centuries: through the oeuvre that I want to build, I will make a great name for us, for those of my own blood, so dear, who abandoned me that winter night two years ago; to drunken Noah mocked by his sons; to Isaac deceived, fathers humiliated, oh my father, kneeling before me, so alone, from two in one, from one in two, reduced to one in one...our mother's ghost within him!

Will I sleep, tears welling up in my eyes, birds whistling already in the seaside dew? I go to the Psalms—enough with stories, figures, enigmatic wrestlings—to a single psalm whose internal utterance, no matter where, has salved my tears since I ceased to believe entirely: "One thing have I desired of the Lord, that will I seek after; that I may dwell in the house of the Lord all the days of my life..."; I pull the sheet over my face to cover my tears, my sobs that, downstairs, unsleeping, he might hear; but for fear that my tears might soak the sheets, I sit up, get out of bed, and go to the sink to cry my fill, my toes tickled at the touch of the busy cockroaches—like the toes of the loyal Hebrews, young and old, asleep on the sand under the still pure sky, tickled by the little desert animals and by the finger of God as he counts them, his people forever.

A large owl cries out, ruffles its vermin-filled wings, and, wise creature with wrathful eye, mindful of its little ones, lice-infested, mucked with filth to their blinking eyes, makes for its nest in the violet predawn light, its sure flight unhindered by the tremors of explosions.

The "Sphynx"

THE NEXT day, I rejoin my army mates at the hotel already partly abandoned by its European staff, and follow them as they join up with other soldiers from regiments of the south: a few of them lead us off—on the way back I already won't know which way we went—to the "Sphynx," where, in a high-vaulted inner rotunda-courtyard, elevators raise and lower subordinate officers, commissioned officers, desk soldiers, red-faced, pressed against the panels by half-naked women, blond Europeans, brunette natives, black Africans, slender Eurasians, breasts bared, pelvises sequined.

The crowd pushes us against a painted wall of the rotunda that rings with raucous cries, elevator machinery; I cling to shoulders that cling to those in front: but a hand, ringed, oiled, fondles me, unbuttons the fly of my off-duty trousers, slips inside, takes hold of my member in my boxer shorts, pulls it out; I draw back, but a mouth, rouged, hot, creviced, joins the hand; a tongue strikes my upraised member, envelops its circumcised head; a tooth touches my frenum, lingers along the scar of the circumcision; new arrivals push me toward the wall—I can't see the girl's face, but only an ear passing, perfumed, from one jacket flap to the other; I don't move, for fear that a motion might make my outstretched member ejaculate—for two years now, because of the lack of privacy, I haven't been able to put it to use to write the first draft of the text that my imagination calls me to—and I want to keep it taut for the Liberation. At eye level, the faces of a few of us go slack; of what material is the fake tooth that pulls away from my turned-back flesh made? Gold for those whose smudged, repainted faces knock against the panes of the elevators rising packed with decorated torsos, gallooned shoulders: the more expert the girl, the more precious her tooth-metal; for those down below, against the walls (the rank and file), it's lead.

Outside, the cold grips my shoulders; I can feel my member, flayed, bleeding; the entire next day, along the sea shore, I walk between my army mates, fever down my spine: we no longer take the streets that penetrate the interior of the upper city, casbah, government-general, universities; we would be a target for both sides there; families come and go along the seafront; sirens, horns, fishing boats, pleasure boats, cargo ships, steamers, departing troops, train whistles; old men and women stare at the sea, the horizon; the night still falls early and quick; newspaper headlines in kiosks announce an imminent cease-fire; the eateries light up, grills blaze, sardines, merguez, broil; children, farther on, shake the turbid water off their naked bodies as they spring from the sea; others, noses pinched, leap into it; one of them re-emerges, a little octopus in his fist.

We come back at curfew to the hotel room shared by five of us, overlooking the oil lamps of the square; I sleep fully dressed except for my jacket, on a bedside rug figured with a hunting scene, beneath a blanket; in the damp night, I awake to half-track treads rolling on tarmac; I step out of the room, go downstairs with my jacket around my shoulders; in the darkened reception office, where a ray of moonlight passes through the pane, a girl lies asleep on a low armchair; and yet she's a woman: her belly is pregnant beneath the two flaps of a partly opened white shirt, the upper lace edges of which rub against her red nipples in the twofold breathing of the mother and gestating child; a pair of slightly swollen legs poke from a short black skirt; I step back into the dark: the door to the square half opens; the sound of the treads receding into the distance intensifies, along with the smell of the port; a young man, plaid shirt open upon a strong chest, bulging-pocketed jeans, steps forward, rifle on his shoulder, his hand, blackened, on the strap; I search for a sound to align with the sound of my breathing; are my bare feet, on the floor, out of the glare? I don't dare to glance at them, for fear that tilting my head might cause my skull, my hair to catch a ray of moonlight; with the rifle swinging to and fro on the shoulder, the blackened hands—blood under the nails, blood between the fingers?—lay themselves upon the two breasts, bared; the young man's head rubs against the woman's head; his mouth takes hold of hers; a sound of kissing, of saliva mingling, sucked...the young man's pelvis tips toward the young woman's radiant breast; half-darkness envelops the whole couple; I hear the sound of a belt, of snaps popping open, of saliva re-swallowed, cheeks slapping, tongues licking; the armchair creaks to the movements of the pelvis; a long groan, then others, shorter; the rifle slips onto the arm, the elbow; the buttstock falls, drags along the tiles; if he saw me, would he kill me, as he kills "Arabs," by day, by night? At the least, wouldn't he point his gun at me to test me, to prove to himself that the conscripts from the home country didn't defend him and his fellows, the French of Algeria? He takes a cartridge clip from his pocket, loads his automatic rifle, makes for the door he left half-open, passes through it with his rifle held straight out in front, and disappears in the night now lightening into blue to the long blast of a horn: a steamer turning in the port, toward the opening of the harbor? The child, whose mother's saliva mingled with its father's seed now... where will it be born, if born at all? On this side of the sea or on the other? The air, having entered through the reclosing door, sends a shiver down her nipples, which she, slack-mouthed, covers with the hem of her soiled shirt, whose folds the dawn now dapples with blue. Did he only caress her groin which the full pregnancy makes it difficult to enter? She hums an air half French lullaby, half Andalusian chant, and caresses with a single finger that organ I have not yet touched, and that I will not believe in until I have put my finger into it, my fingers—one wouldn't suffice—my mouth.

He, with his unsleeping band of fighters: Is he lying in ambush in some nook of street waste, bicycles, scaffoldings, to wait there, take aim at the first Arab-looking laborers, workers, and fire? Until a salvo of bullets brings him down, fired from some darkened window where the lace curtain hardly twitches, or from the turret of a tank on sentry duty, after shouted warnings?

Interrogation

AT THE signal-transmission table in the company barracks, the approaches to which have been reinforced with sandbags, we take shifts receiving the ceasefire messages, the orders concerning its enforcement; captains, officers stand waiting, up above, on the balcony of the manor house of the old farm requisitioned at the outset of the insurrection; a few more bottles than usual to uncap on the table where the flies zizz and drone over the scraps of black meat; those of us who kept watch all night in front of the crackling devices now wake on straw mattresses, from what nightmares of military service prolongations?

We can sense that—with the factions now reinforced by others, no longer suppressed by the urgency of the eleventh-hour combats—mutilations, murders, rapes, acts of torture, massacres are being prepared throughout the entire territory. And, without saying a word, we sense that our having received the text of the ceasefire makes us complicit in it, complicit in France's surrender, in its—diplomatic—defeat, its betrayal of its army, victorious on the ground, and the as good as planned abandonment of the Algerians who were loyal to France.

Snow still lies among the rocks of the high coastal forest where officers of the French army must guarantee the safe passage of resistance fighters from out of caves where, a few days earlier, they would have blasted them out with mines; in the command car of the captain—who has taken this route in accordance with I don't know what order, not issued through my radio—I await, in a clearing warmed by the full sun crisscrossed by the flights of buzzards, the end of the conclaves: in a notebook on my knee, I write the short, majestic opening passage of a future book; as the captain, off apart, speaks with others standing beneath the firs, a senior officer, short, surly-faced beneath his beret, sets his elbows on the command-car hood and, in a sharp voice, asks me what I am writing: the composition of the text having rekindled my civilian "I" that my subjection had damped, I scrawl another line and, without according him the required salute, even from my seat, I ask him, as if waking from some beautiful dream that has been interrupted, why it takes several officers to supervise the departure of resistance fighters who, given the status quo established by the ceasefire, could just as well have found their way home on their own; I see his face puff out, turn red, his mouth mutter; I hear him threaten me, order me to step out of the vehicle; the captain—to whom I lend the newspapers I receive from one of my mother's sisters, imprisoned at Fresnes during the Occupation and now committed to the cause of Algerian independence—comes back over to us and enjoins me to comply; rage lifts my ribs in my chest; my radio hisses, crackles; I am being called from below; I have to listen to the message, tap out the reply; the senior officer, muttering, walks away, but I hear him shout that I haven't heard the last from him. At the far end of the clearing, rebels who last night would have been shot as enemy combatants come out from their stronghold, arms raised and song at their lips.

Later in the month, higher in the mountains, at the end of a new mine-clearing mission, I start to disassemble my signal station; the radio crackles; Morse signals pour in; I can't understand them; then, at my request, the signals come with longer pauses; I understand from them that danger awaits me down below; the lieutenant is worried to see my worry, but how, coming from the captain's quarters of the resettlement camp outpost, could he be unaware of a measure that concerns one of his men, and the one entrusted with coded communications at that?

I learn that one of our fellow soldiers, a *Français de Souche Nord-Africain*, a "North African French soldier" assigned to our offices, with whom I am friendly, and whom, when I saw him worried about his fate after the planned independence, I advised to enlist in the "Force Locale"—the ratified, official institution for the transfer of power—instead deserted to the National Liberation Army last night and made threats against soldiers of our commando unit as he did so.

Down below, as I step from the jeep with part of my equipment in my arms, I see three empty command cars, with their drivers leaning against them, in the small courtyard in front of the command post; above, on the balcony, gold glitters in the opening of the French door to the captain's office; I step, with my little dog, to the side of the entrance, slip into a familiar passageway of barbed wire crushed between collapsed stone pillars, and enter our barracks from the back; my army mates, quick, inform me that I am about to be arrested, that my locker has been emptied, that the drivers, upon arriving, warned them of the search, and that they have concealed a few of my papers—the prologue to a forthcoming novel I wrote in the command car—with the personal items of the corporal, an apprentice pastry chef in civilian life, who is about to depart for his liberation to the home country; foreseeing, seeing, fore-suffering that I am about to disappear into some military prison, without a trial—a trial? here, in this time of general unrest, of lawlessness, and for me, a common soldier?—I pick up my camera, stand before our mirror, and photograph myself photographing myself, as my little mutt leaps about my legs; my army mates pass each other the camera and one of them stuffs it into his locker; where have the three soldiers with white armbands come from who now enter, shove their feet against the dog who barks at them, and seize hold of me? They push me into the small courtyard where a senior officer, colonel or lieutenant colonel, stands at the balcony tapping the top of his shiny boot with a swagger stick; they push me up the stairs as the colonel steps into the office of the captain who stands at the entrance, his hand saluting at his temple.

Accused, do I still have to salute them, I who, if I were "free," would burst into laughter at these salutes and obligatory forms of address—"*mon capitaine*," "*mon lieutenant*," "*sergeant*," and so forth?

The colonel has taken a seat behind the table on the swivel chair of the captain who separates me from the soldiers and orders me to stand up straight and give the required salute; but already my ear no longer completely hears him; although awake, I am in an immediate future of prison without end: a part of me, flesh and spirit, vanishes into it as a ghost; as a ghost, too, stands the other part of me, in un-straightened field dress, alone, without rights, before two adults endowed with absolute power, and yet I am forced to resist them; I am shapeless clay that circumstances will form into a hardened thing.

The colonel, a fairly tall fifty-year-old man with graying hair, recites the acts, the allegations of my treason, without speaking my name or looking at me. His chest is bedecked with medals whose meaning and significance I do not know—I never, as a child, saw any of them on the clothes of my aunts and uncles, heroes of the French Resistance, even on those of the one who was a survivor of the death camps, or on the mourning card—with the opening of the *Ode to Joy* by Schiller, a German, as its text—of the one who disappeared at the age of twenty-three in the death camp, with gas chamber, crematorium, human-experiments laboratory, of Oranienburg-Sachsenhausen. Rising from his chair, the colonel takes a little notebook out of his left pocket, opens it, and, pulling his glasses from his right pocket, reads out phrases in which, after two pages, a familiar inflection reaches me through the ringing in my ears: my "style," notes of mine, therefore, from a pad the army mates didn't have time to hide; the colonel gives the hint of a hand movement to accompany the rhythm; further on, he begins a note and, looking up at the captain who snaps to attention, tells him that the note is about him, that I have written there that he reminds me at once of some auburn youth of Stendhal's, with a naive, tenebrous charm, and of a figure of Thomas Hardy's, bent under some secret, fatal social burden; as the captain remains standing at attention with the flat of his hand at his temple, the two ghosts within me shake with laughter that my mouth suppresses: Does the army snap to attention thus at one of my sentences? But I can also hear that the further the army advances in my "profile," the more the motives of the accusation against me become clear, and, along with them, the colonel's pleasure at having caught one of those intellectuals, however slight, who have prevented the army from keeping Algeria for France and Western civilization, and are instead allowing it to deliver itself up to international communism.

The quotations finished, including a number of rumors I have heard and written down concerning exactions committed and claimed by the commandos of our and other companies—rapes, ears cut from corpses and sent in packages to the home country—the colonel stands up, sets his manicured hands on the table and states that, for these quoted passages, for my repeated acts of rebellion, my incitations to protest, the possession and distribution of prohibited pamphlets and newspapers, and as an accessory to desertion and to the deserter's threats against the commandos—for which, if he acts upon them, I will be held accountable—the totality of which constitutes the crime of corrupting the morale of the army, he hereby inculpates me on the spot and orders the captain to imprison me forthwith in solitary confinement, and informs me that tomorrow morning I will be transported to regional headquarters for investigations preliminary to trial. Clicking heels, effluvia of aftershave, at-attentions in the small courtyard, jeeps starting up.

Alone with the captain in his office, as he sits at his table again, his head in his hands, and laments "what a nice mess" I've got myself into, I ask him to help me get out of it; his torment at seeing his company tainted by a quasi-shameful accusation is—I can tell by the hint of a smile he flashes me as he lifts his head—allayed by what the colonel read aloud from my note about him: he would like to hear more about it.

But I am eager to be alone; and so he has me remove my shoelaces, my belt, empty my pockets; seeing that my fatigues are bloodied at the calf and knee—I cut myself on some barbed wire in the village—he offers to have them bandaged; I tell him that the saliva of my little dog will be enough to disinfect and heal the wounds; he has me go down with a sergeant into the corridor between the command post and our signal-transmission room; on the right, toward the broad assembly courtyard, the commando barracks, the mess hall, the watchtowers, a large door opens onto a high-ceilinged storage closet; they lock me in it, with the dog, but only for tonight; no dinner, but some of my barrack mates, until lights-out, knock at the locked door and murmur a few of our familiar expressions; my little dog, each time I startle out of sleep, leaps onto the pile of blankets, worn, moldy, that I've made, and licks at my bared leg.

At dawn, the door unlocks; a sergeant to whom my army mates have given my toiletries leads me to the back of the broad courtyard, to the water trough of the old farm, in front of the Machine hangar at the edge of the camp; I walk shuffling my laceless combat boots and holding my fatigues up at the waist; I wash up, shave without a mirror: I am not allowed to possess glass, which, broken, I could use to harm myself, kill myself; my eyeglasses will be confiscated each night; this morning, before my first interrogation—did I prepare for it, or did I dream my replies?—I look into the dark-green water where the blue is shifting into rose and see tadpoles wriggling between the mosses; where are the frogs and toads? Did they simply, under the cover of a downpour, hop from the bog beneath the watchtower—atop which, when I wasn't in the field, I did my repeated shifts of guard duty—into the water, always so clear, to reproduce there without a partner? If I let my face linger there, it's to study the face I have in it, all childlike, before desire: all curiosity, liveliness, cunning, audacity; to make myself the face I have to show my questioners, my enemies.

A sergeant presses me forward, pushes me into a jeep where a helmeted officer with a white armband is seated beside the driver; the jeep leaves the town center where a few men grown old before their time stand shaking out tattered clothes; the jeep drives onward in the risen day; I know the prefecture capital isn't far, but I imagine obstacles, temporary detours, to prolong this advance along a gentle slope toward a place whose name I have not been told: checkpoints, an ambush even, from whatever faction, in which to escape and find shoelaces and a belt; we pass below a place called Guynemer, named after the World War I aviator hero whose letters from the front I read as a child: I am seized with rage at these figures of French military heroism who now condemn me, and whose names, often blood-steeped, still designate cities old and new in this territory where, as I well know, those who detain me will be driven out in the season to come—but prison has no national boundaries.

Along the edge of a small military camp near the road, soldiers bustle about beside little mounds of cigarette cartons in flames; instruments, tools, utensils, underwear, socks, shoes, jackets, overcoats, pants, berets, bedcovers, gathered into heaps among the Barbary figs, will soon be thrown into the flames before the eyes of farmers driven from their lands and regrouped in rectilinear towns; nothing must be left behind for those who have rejected us, and as the army has a precise quota of loss, of waste, the operation takes place in broad daylight.

In the prefecture capital, the crowd, among whom I cast about for eyes whose bodies might free me from my jailers, attends to the stalls: disemboweled animals, violet entrails, hang there, turn in the half-darkness where butchers shiver in the morning dew, large knives and cleavers in their fists. A clicking of weapons, of cartridges loaded into chambers; the jeep accelerates into a red-dirt curve under eucalyptus trees, cedars whose scent descends upon me, protects me like a cloud over a people in flight; the jeep stops at the entrance checkpoint, I hear slack voices exchanging words about me, but as if in a foreign tongue; the jeep rolls farther ahead, passes along flowerbeds edged with white: the space is swarming with more officers than I have seen in a year and a half of service; the combat officers stand out distinctly from the desk officers.

How will I step out of the jeep without my combat boots slipping from my feet? How place my feet in them and hold my fatigues up at the same time? Will they let me keep these military clothes I am now unworthy of wearing?

I step out; it all holds; I am pushed through glass doors, along an Ottoman-tiled hall, into a concrete staircase under construction, upstairs into a long corridor lined with office bays. The officer, unhelmeted, ushers me into one room, empty; then into another, filled with unbuttoned soldiers rummaging through boxes; then into another where, beneath a lampshade that he switches off, an officer sits leafing through documents; with a weary motion of his hand, he repels us back into the corridor; the soldiers come out of the previous office, dragging their feet; which side are they on? At the last office in the corridor, which continues beyond a door guarded by an orderly—Makarov pistol at his breast, strap around his neck—they keep me standing as an hour passes on the great clock in the main courtyard; we enter a large room with ornamental moldings; two desks, one of them large, with gleaming wood, two telephones in the light of the bay windows; the other desk in the half-darkness to the right of the entrance, a telephone receiver on Formica; calendars hang from the yellow walls, all crossed out up to yesterday, and so I can read on them what day it is, which, last night on the moldy pile of blankets, I struggled to recall.

As I stand dazzled by the sun that they refuse to allow me to step out of, a lieutenant enters and, without looking at me, sits at the small desk; if the accusing colonel has kept his word, then that must be him the guard now salutes with great fanfare at the entrance: here he is, swagger stick in hand, something on his head, stripes on his high shoulders, medals glinting, each of his words, gestures, motions, intestinal rumblings is an order, an accusation, a threat, a taunt. As he passes through the door—the lieutenant stands at attention—he veers to his left, knocks into me; he flings his gloves onto the desk, one falls to the floor where his orderly, a young redhead, retrieves it; the colonel hands him his hat which he sets down at the edge of the large desktop; the colonel takes a seat there in a beautiful swivel chair, looks at me from below; I see him lift his booted right leg onto his left knee; both boots shine all the way down to their soles; leaning back in his chair, he waits for the lieutenant to bring him a string-fastened folder that he unknots with a sigh: from atop the pages appears the little green volume of my first published book, which he had his men seize from my locker with a part of my notes; still on my feet, without laces or belt, no coffee no bread in my stomach, will I have to hear and justify each phrase I have written in my little work of fiction and notes? I hear them make plans for a ten-day interrogation; the lieutenant will take charge of the factual, material notes; the colonel of the notes of political and psychological judgment, and of the little book that, sliding one boot over the other, he already begins to leaf through; his lips follow along with his reading; my heart pounds in fear that they will open upon a voice speaking the phrases in which I have captured a part of my first bloom of love, whose figures my probable destruction in prison will prevent me from ever tempering and fathoming in a true adult work of fiction; but his lips do open; my phrases, which he pronounces in a sharp voice, give out a little freshness in the confined space: the balance of their rhythm, their vigor, and their irony come through his throat in spite of himself: he carries on with his reading in silence; the lieutenant recites a note in which I describe the physical misery of the troops: fatigues in tatters, filthy bodies, vermin, rotten food, fellow soldiers stationed at a certain outpost where one of them lost his mind, machine-gunned, from the top of the watchtower, imaginary rebels in the adjoining outposts; the colonel cuts him off, raises a finger, reads out a paragraph, stops short at an ellipsis that he considers too daring, reproaches me for it; I justify it; hunger makes me stand up straight. All the way to evening—while they are away at lunch in the mess hall, the clamor of which I can hear, a seated sergeant guards me while I stand, then I sit while he stands—they question me in turn; as the lieutenant reads my notes aloud, I correct, augment, amplify them inwardly—I rediscover the pleasure I took in writing them, and the certitude that the intellect is inviolable, even the fragile intellect of so young a man as I—but my lips are moving; the colonel watches me transform the note I made; as a reader, he must suppose I'm doing it to dig deeper, to castigate the commanding officers' contempt, their negligence, darken the strokes; but, carrying on with his reading, he calls upon the lieutenant and the officers and subordinate officers passing in the corridor to witness each coarse or sexual thing he might find in the little piece of fiction written in several voices that he reads aloud to them: these vivid, crude little passages, which he reads in an artificially lascivious tone, as he would a piece of bourgeois erotica, cause the officers to whistle and hiss, and the soldiers, conscripts, and bureaucrats who accompany them whistle as well, but at a higher pitch. Once a cutthroat's accomplice, I now pass for a pornographer. I, who already reject all erotic interpretations of the little I have written at the time, what am I supposed to answer to their whistlings? Hungry, holding up my uniform, now too big at my waist grown thin from the last campaigns and the shock of my arrest, I cannot, in my still embarrassed youth, act the part of an author who is master of his lasciviousness; and if, reading further on, he comes to phrases that prove my virginity, of which he seems to be informed from my mainland service file—my repeated rebellions, the un-love letter from my darling in Paris—will he cast it all up before my face to those now crowding at the door to his office? The preliminary investigation of my case is supposed to be kept secret—and I am to be kept without counsel, and not even informed of my rights—but here, and for such people as these, might is right, all the more since they were forced, during the putsch, to submit themselves to right, and they are having their little revenge here; but the colonel—whose tone of voice and manners might lead one to believe that, here in the prefecture capital, he perhaps frequents a private club to which the current circumstances have restored the luster and cruelty of its finest days, and that he may have learned there that the publisher of my little volume, though complicit in the decolonization, is one of the most renowned publishers in Paris—seizes upon their hints of sarcasm and makes them desist; and by having refused to "bury" the gravity, and spuriousness, of the accusations against me with a bawdy acknowledgment of the soldiers' arousal, I have preserved the honor of my little work and of the French language, which, since early adolescence, I have aspired to renew; he closes the little book, shuffles through the confiscated notes, takes out a leaflet, reads it, tells me, sotto voce but in front of those who remain at the door, that I have a very active imagination, which I am aware of—and the nerves that go with it too—and that, in the following days, I will have to justify each of the facts reported in these notes, and that soldiers from the implicated units will be brought down from the village.

They take me back to my company, to my storage closet; the captain has a plate of black meat and beans brought to me; my little dog is returned to me while I eat—with neither knife nor fork—the army mates crowd at the door, bare-chested, bring me clean underlinen; lying on the heap of blankets, I stare at the ceiling of this former quartermaster's store where the beam of our watchtower's spotlight passes before a high opening: bats brush past the timbers there; the wounds on my leg, disinfected by the mutt's valiant tongue, begin to heal; standing in place has frayed my nerves, I jump up, hang from a low wooden rafter; I run a circle in the small dark space, the forms of which I recognize only by the odor they give off; this exercise which I force myself to do—and will continue to force myself to do in the days to come, despite the anguish that catches me in the throat until I can hardly breathe and have to seek some position to relieve it, lying down, standing, crouching, hanging—is exercise that I have done since I was a child, when, from my mother's mouth or from my earliest readings, I first learned of the daily routines in the death camps, roll calls, beatings, humiliations, hunger, thirst, colic, and I began to refer each little torment of my little life to them, to reduce its intensity and its consequences, to accept it and pass beyond it: here, it's the confinement in the cattle wagons, the seclusion in a space hardly bigger than the body, in a cellar pit, days, weeks, months without light, walled in—Antigone (I am she, in mind, in will, to my father blinded by grief).

At sunrise, earlier and more vivid in spring, me already loaded into the jeep, the army mates give me coffee straight from the ladle that they dip in the pot; on the way to the prefecture capital, a checkpoint, civilian police—a massacre higher in the mountains—since they have a military prisoner on their hands, my jailers pass through; at the

General Staff offices, the colonel and the lieutenant seem harsher than yesterday: Have they received death threats? The interrogation comes to the core of the matter: I am one of those who, since the First Indochina War, either communist or Christian hoodwinked by communists, have protested against and denounced the army's efforts to maintain France in possession of her colonies, which have cost her dearly but which she has had the courage to safeguard against the "Soviets," and perhaps also against the still distant, menacing shadow of an Islam renewed in its fanaticism. Will I be able to hold firm within me what I know of the Algerian insurgency, from its texts and the actions of some of its precursors, and what I know of the spectacle of misery—the little mounds of food waste ringed round with children and old men and women foraging with hooks for something to eat—the cruelty of the Conquest and of the Repression, and how, everywhere, behind the facade of the often ignorant joviality of their fellow citizens of European descent, the non-European Algerians, rich and poor alike, having become French citizens, stand as strangers in the land of their fathers.

From the far end of the corridor, a group of soldiers and subordinate officers come forward, carrying in their arms a pale young soldier, his blue eyes shifting from horror to half-sleep, his arm slackened against the hardened arms of his temporary porters: his torso is clothed in only a khaki undershirt; his legs shake with tremors; while the colonel, whose authority would be compromised by even a mere glance at such a miserable subordinate, reexamines my sheaf of notes, Bic pen in his fingers and at his jaw, the lieutenant introduces me to this young soldier—to whom I, as a fellow conscript, feel closer than the lieutenant, an enlisted man, believes himself to be—and says that he is a victim of those whose cause I support and of whose atrocities I therefore approve; and, moreover, that it is only decency that keeps him from telling me the cause of this man's agony... Does he want me to believe that my "friends" have castrated this poor soldier? With my toes curled in my laceless combat boots, I step toward the lieutenant who rises to his feet and steps backward in the half-light, a paperweight in his hand; the colonel stands up, lays his hand on the swagger stick lying at the corner of the desk; does he want to come round and strike me with it? Or humiliate his underling by stepping in to defend him? The fighter—of lost wars—teaching the police bureaucrat a lesson. I step farther forward; in the corridor the porters grow excited; the prospect of a physical confrontation between this lieutenant, who is from a colonial family, and me diminishes their hostility toward the one who they have been told is a traitor. Seeing the swagger stick shine in the colonel's fist, I step to his desk, stretch forth my arm above it toward the sheaf of my little yellow notepad; the lieutenant, coming from the half-light, seizes my other arm; attempting to hold up my pants, which are falling down, I allow him to seize the arm whose hand has reached the pad; he tugs me backward with his flabby limbs, returns me to my place; at a sign from the colonel, he sits me down on a little bench between two piles of folders; the group has left the corridor; I feel the blood withdraw from the veins in my arms and legs; dried spittle between my teeth; I draw in long breaths; my vision darkens, but I can see a glass approach my face, with a little bit of pink liquid slapping at the sides: Who is it who moves the edge of the glass toward my mouth, forces it past my lips? Lie back? Bench too narrow; on the ground? What could I do there, say there, to keep my dignity or humor? What can I fix my thoughts on, to hold out, sitting at least, not lose consciousness? To keep my rage intact, and the rightness of my cause? On the wounded soldier's pale face—a noble pallor; my own pallor, even from wrath, pleases them well, as it attests to the feebleness of my nerves, and therefore of my reasoning, even if they are already familiar with my arguments, incontrovertible and therefore constantly bandied about; but anxious about their own careers, and familiar with the medical file from my conscription, perhaps they fear that the news of my fainting fit might spread through the division, and that this loss of consciousness could force them to hospitalize me?

Imagining the worst—in thought his face almost directly facing mine—for this child-man sent to war, illegally, as a minor, while I, beside him, turn to face once more my two interrogators, nearer now, their buttocks against the desk, I gather my breath and blood; the rising warmth of both together brings tears to the corner of my eyes; compared to his wounded, mutilated body, of what consequence is this judicial inquiry, me unmaimed and my little book before me in their hands? Compared to the ennui that awaits him, farmer or craftsman or factory man deprived of his profession, of women—whereas I can invent them with words as I will—deprived of children, whereas I can people my tales to come with the most beautiful, the most miserable ones of all...

The reading of my notes resumes in the afternoon, after a plate of beans brought by a fellow soldier whose impetigo-infected nose drips snot into them; for some of the notes in which, starting from an event reported by army mates in the adjacent units, I have sketched out a scene that prolongs and harshens it, already with figures augmented, I must answer to their origin without giving up the names of the sources; detach the elaborations from the original information, affirm that, wanting to write, having already written and been published, I am not here in this war as an informant or even as a witness, and that what he, the colonel, now holds in his gloved hands is private—like the love letters—and that, as they monitor all correspondence, they cannot even accuse me of passing information to the mainland; that it is their own handling of these work-notes that has rendered them public; would they expect of me that, as a soldier, I cease all inner, all spiritual activity?—from several clues I have realized that they are nonbelievers, and I say the word to confound them, for I know the army is anxious to be respectful of religious beliefs, just as it is respectful of social condition; as an "intellectual," in their eyes—I who, at the time, hardly know the word—I would be more harshly treated than one of the uneducated from whom they expect full submission.

Commentary by commentary, my faith in Algeria's independence alternately falters and gathers strength; today, in the presence of the army, which is duty-bound to defend the Republic—all the more so during this spring in which the army is to guarantee an accord that will dismember the Republic's territory—and in the presence of the army tribunal, I am aware of the strength of words, even of such still fragile words as mine, and the responsibility borne by the one who chooses these words—twin powers that I have come to know through my clandestine adolescent writings and through the other, public, writings that torment my father; and, entirely alone, caught between my notes which the colonel puts forth with sarcastic or honeyed voice and the armed national authorities, between my naked works and the massacres forecasted for summer, defenseless, with no support "network," cut off from all correspondence, from all newspapers and magazines, with my army mates' letters monitored, who or what am I to call upon to reinforce my convictions, when, on top of it all, I know that, as neither an Algerian nor a European of Algeria, but only, just barely, a French citizen, I can claim the right to speak of these convictions only from a moral perspective—and what right at all, for that matter, when I have lived so little?

The discussion turns to the leaders of the Algerian insurrection; to the March accords in which Krim Belkacem is the chief negotiator for the Algerian side: the colonel eases back in his armchair, stretches his booted legs out beneath the double desk, throws back his head, puffs on an imaginary cigar, and tilts his slender hand with his gloves between his fingers above his upraised arm: "Krim? Why, when he was with us, he used to shine my boots!" I can't repress a smile, and then nearly hysterical laughter; the colonel lays his hand on the desk again, draws in his boots: in wanting to diminish his former orderly—before me, who am touched to the core by these destinies that span from the lowest to the highest—he has just magnified him by recalling that, fifteen years ago, as a subordinate officer, the cosignatory of the abdication of one of the mightiest colonial empires in history used to shine the boots of a captain who, today, is not even a general.

Another nine days of interrogations, coercions, brief staged appearances of fellow soldiers wounded in the village. The trip each morning is too short, too easy: an ambush, a chance to escape there; I could surely find a pair of shoes abandoned on the banks of an oued or in a gorge, to lace up my boots again, a belt, civilian clothes; tracked, on the run again, I could come to an arrangement with any one of the factions.

On the trip back to the company, I fill my eyes with light; locked up in the high storage closet, I readjust my pupils to the dark; lying on the pile of blankets, I wait for the silence that follows curfew, to listen to nothing but the flight of the bats—are there only two, or more?—and fall asleep; the next evening, the height of the ceiling transforms me into a figure on the set of Victor Sjöström's film *The Wind*; I assume the gestures, the pantomimes of the principal characters and speak their intertitled words to them, wife, husband; despite my anguish, melodies, musical motifs, come through my throat, then later my mouth; I reconstruct entire pieces, brief, for piano, for voice and piano, then later for orchestra, more and more complex, variations, developments; in the dark, I slip into large and less large paintings in the Louvre, lay my hand on the draperies, the cloths that hang from Veronese's tables, the gleaming objects, hide myself away in the wheat fields of Poussin's *The Summer*, nestle against the donkey in Watteau's *Gilles*, receive upon my face the blood of the Turkish cavalrymen in *The Massacre at Chios*; my little mutt no longer scratches at the door; an army mate about to be discharged has taken him with him and will bring him to my father in the home country; they are crossing, at this moment, the Mediterranean.

If a fire starts in the company's main building, will someone remember to unlock the storeroom for me?

The roads and streets grow empty; everyone keeps to their houses, on watch; the shopkeepers lower their metal shutters early; heads, everywhere, turn side to side, behind, above, below; but on the reeking mounds circled by birds of prey that the spring has roused from their nests, old women and children in rags hook their rotten offal from among the scraps of vomit.

Solitary Confinement

ONE MORNING, the hour to leave for the General Staff offices slips past; at noon, army mates open the door, take me to wash at the watering trough, then, under the smiling eyes of the captain, through the large courtyard to the camp's east exit where the jeep from the staff offices usually parks, but they push me gently on toward the kitchens, where fellow soldiers with bared red chests churn black meat and beans in large pots on coal fires where I can see the white-hot shards; before the entrance to the kitchens, a stone stairway—facing a perpetual rubbish heap of vegetable and meat scraps from which a mixture of juice, grease, and blood seeps along the concrete toward the slab at the top of the stairs—descends to a cellar shut with a thick-barred iron door: the daytime officer of the guard opens it with a large key; the space isn't as narrow as the storage closet, but the vault, sweating, is low; the walls are made of small stones covered in moss, the domed floor of hard-packed dirt; facing the door is a mattress—of sawdust, I can smell it—on the bare ground; an army mate from our barracks brings me some spare khaki underclothes, a blanket; will I be interrogated again tomorrow?

The officer of the guard shows me—against regulation—his order book: bring me out in the mornings under watch with loaded rifle, *shoot in case of attempted escape*; each directive is written in red, underlined. I learn from my army mates that I have been sentenced to three months in prison, *solitary confinement*. The door shuts in my face.

Except in the case of thunderstorm and of runoff on the steps and floor, I am required to keep my sawdust mattress in front of the door; all afternoon I inspect the walls, where a few loose stones might serve as hiding places.

The shadows of the army cooks pass to and fro at the top of the steps; I hear a kind of sob: Is it from the one whose fiancée abandoned him in a letter, and upon whom the army mates heap obscenities?

That same sob, very brief, was also my own, a day ago, midway through the interrogation session, when the colonel took out a letter from one of my mother's sisters—imprisoned in Fresnes during the Occupation, now supporting and hiding Algerians committed to the insurrection, indignant that France should send such very young soldiers to risk forfeiting their souls in the military crackdown—waved the letter, flattened it out on his desk, and mocked its simple Christian words...

Having held out for nine days, I faltered the instant of that sob— which, falling suddenly silent, the two officers took for surrender.

And don't I reproach myself for it, here in the gathering darkness of the prison cell? Humiliation, doubt seize me entirely: if only I had them in front of me, the two humans, my elders, to find again each time my taste for answering back, to dare to protest, even to speak the words, the names of insurrection and war that the chain of command forbids us to use. But what right do I have, unwounded, to assert the due rights of armed insurgents? Newly minted citizen of an afflicted Republic, what right do I have to be already scribbling little sketches of "irresponsible" fiction against her?

My rage at having possibly yielded, or having at least given them that illusion, keeps me on my feet; I explore the ground that will be my lot for three months, tap at it with heel and toe: all spaces have a drain; I search for it; at the back corners, empty bottles roll beneath my feet: an old wine cellar; I don't recall the captain ever locking up one of our own in here—the prison for drunkenness and other offenses is in the guardhouse: they want to separate me from the rest of the company, hide me as deep as they can.

Between dinner and lights-out, in the long light of the setting sun, army mates come from our barracks, scantily dressed, and sit or crouch on the steps, to watch me eat my plateful; one of them brings me the remains of a little expired account book found in the kitchen and a small pencil whose lead I will have to use frugally; I put them under one of the loose stones at the base of the wall; eating, with my plate on my knees, as they sit before me, half-naked, skin, faces, eyes shining, I feel as if we were slaves, gladiators, or wild beasts waiting, ill-fated and merry, for the whip that will wake us to a morning of bloodshed.

The officer of the guard, when the others are gone, comes down and opens the door to search the bedding, the corners, my clothes, me; three times during the night, he comes down without opening up, shines his flashlight on me in bed under the vaulted ceiling—on which I can then see insects, worms. Some scurry and wriggle on the dirt floor: How to keep them away from my mattress on the bare dirt? The next morning, an army mate from the night watch hands me through the bars a bottle of liquid repellent that I pour onto the ground around my mattress.

Doubt, shame, rage keep me awake; I detach the little stone at the base of the wall, take out the orange-colored pad, and, below the remnants of accounts, of kilos, I write a first note: *Nothing is pure*; not them, not me, especially not me; nobody to confirm me in what remains of my self; the certitude of a few facts: the imminent independence of a people that has claimed its due rights; my desire to create; between these two realities, one collective, the other personal, I am nothing; even my body escapes me; my nerves constrain its movements; and that brief sob during the last interrogation: how I wish I could go back in time, as in the case of the theft, and live the scene again to my advantage—or rather, to the advantage of the Cause that they associate me with, whose collective strength my individual weakness has perhaps diminished.

One afternoon, when I can hear the outbursts of a little party among the platoons, as I lie on my sawdust mattress that grows damp with humidity, I see the shadows of dark clouds passing quickly over the stone steps beyond the thick bars where, on one, a large snail clings, having climbed from a few tufts of grass at the foot of the stairs: as in the fields of Wessex, where Jude and Sue walk trailing their sex and the refusal of sex; I try to reconstruct a grand scene from Thomas Hardy's *Jude the Obscure*, with thunderstorm, meadow, hillside village, door knocker of a socially banished house, social fate, latent infanticide.

But Jude and Sue, however hobbled by the fate that their times have laid upon them, are still so human, living through weighty passions, worthy of supreme Judgment, whereas I, locked up, only just recently lifted out of a passive and reckless, tormented and merry adolescence by adults who are ranking officers, decorated, assured of promotion, and whom I cannot yet conceive of as my fellow citizens, me, unworthy of a trial, even a military one, pitiful quarry of well-practiced military police, abandoned—at least, I haven't had the slightest word from him—by a captain to whom I had offered my friendship, whom I had lent my rare newspapers, pamphlets—I am no longer even in possession of my pads of notes and sketches, from which I derive my identity, the proof that I am alive.

Thunder, flashes of lightning, a sudden, sharp odor of vegetation, water, earth, stone, of the cooks slumbering on their straw mattresses up above; the downpour lashes the peneplain, the piles of pots waiting to be scoured in the small courtyard; the wind twists the branches of the eucalyptus trees; the party—a few Gloria Lasso tunes and, already, those of a certain Johnny Hallyday whom the army mates listen to on Saturday nights, their transistor radios dialed to "Petit Bal," their languid bodies stretched out on their straw mattresses—grows louder than ever, volume cranked against the clatter of the thunderstorm: Are they dancing already, twined in each other's arms according to their preferences in grotesque pantomime, tins of mackerel in white wine open on the oilcloth of the communal table, while the signal-transmission equipment crackles in the background?

Have the "cave commandos," reduced now to mine-clearing—those toughs in tight retailored combat uniforms—deigned to mingle with the footsloggers of the Corps of Engineers?

Greasy water cascades down the steps toward the bottom of the bars: How to block its passage? Can the cave fill up like a hole with me inside? Bones from quarters of meat kept in open storerooms to be processed in the kitchens are already rolling in the water that swells, falls from step to step, slaps against the corroded bottom of the bars; the reddened water advances along the earthen floor; I lift my sawdust mattress, press it against the highest point of the cell: Should I dig by hand a channel in the dirt to divert the flow of putrid water directly toward the sides, toward the slope of the domed floor along the walls? At the back, the water would stagnate there, far from any light to dry it up. I dig with my nails, well grown out again—my wrath during the last few days having done its work.

The water, greasy, red, smelling of blood, flows past my fingers.

Outside, the rain subsides, stops; I hear the croaking of frogs in the bog beneath the watchtower; the multicolored gleam of a rainbow spreads through the small courtyard where the pots shine, scattered; the water covers all of the hard-packed earth, soaks the bottom of my sawdust mattress, grows foul already in the corners, laps at the base of the walls from which worms fall.

Combat boots scrape against the soil outside, creak, polished, at the cellar window; I recognize the boots of the commandos: I have been told that one of them, more concerned with showing off his beauty than with cultivating the fruits of his narrow brain, has been informed—by what person with access to my pitiful file?—that one of the notes in my confiscated papers named him as a target of my "North African French" friend who deserted for the National Liberation Army—how could I have written such a note on a pad I no longer had access to?—and that this commando is now out to do me harm and is looking to marshal the help of his platoon mates, commandos whom I accompanied as a radio operator on some of their peacekeeping missions after the ceasefire, and who showed me signs of friendship when I wrote their love letters for them to send to their fiancées, on the verge of slipping into the arms of others; are these combat boots I see accumulating at the cellar window the boots of the commandos he has succeeded in convincing to torment me? I move to a corner close to the cellar window, almost beneath it: on the other side, at the back of the cell, they could see me if they lie flat on their bellies. The rainbow endures and colors even the tops of the combat boots and the hems of their retailored fatigues, but, born and raised in nature, I know the thunderstorm will start again; from the party that the rain's interruption has shifted to the courtyard behind the command post, I hear cranked-up transistor radios, thick cries, pre-vomitory heaves, then, off apart, a sound of barking: the dogs from the outskirts of camp, feral mongrels crossbred with jackals that are themselves half-mixed with house dogs: Have they joined the party to snag scraps of food, or have they been captured to serve as dance partners?

Thunder again, flashes of lightning, rain; the water fills the base of the prison walls again, covers the domed floor: What can I bale or empty it out with? I search, grope about with my fingers: Is there a passage to an under-cell, an oubliette, a private ossuary of one of the farm's original owners? My fingers dig into the slightest cracks they find in the ground, in vain: If the cell floods, will the cooks sleeping off the effects of their wine hear my cries?

At a lull in the downpour, I hear a barking that moves about, comes closer to the cellar window, a long barking as if at the moon; a mass is tugged to the top of the steps, the barking modulates at each twitch of the tugging; as the light dims for another downpour, I see the mass tumble down the steps; it's one of our army mates, the youngest, from a Corps of Engineers platoon, bare-chested, barefoot, his light summer shorts heavy with piss hanging loose at his waist, a leash around his neck as his fresh, childlike face, anxious and laughing, barks at a soon-to-rise moon; the daytime officer of the guard, who is the only one with a key to the cell, his chin covered in vomit, struggles to find the keyhole or padlock; the barred door opened, the body rolls at my feet on the dirt floor; why throw into prison a drunken army mate in a lycanthropic fit who can't stop vomiting? Is he to be cast out from the company like me?

I ask for some water so he can drink and wash his front parts covered in vomit, a basin for him to vomit into; everything is refused me; they tell me they will come and fetch the body tomorrow morning, sobered up; and they relock the cell.

The party has ceased; night begins; the jackals whine in the mountains before the sea; an owl passes over the kitchen; I can hear even her wingbeats, but with the cooks already snoring, she swerves off from the malodorous sector, free toward the town center to fetch there what to feed to her little ones; the army mate, on his knees at the edge of the domed dirt floor, vomits into the flooded channel at the base of the wall; after each spasm, he turns to me where I stand holding my sawdust mattress upright against the wall, beams at me with his merry, luminous face, his faintly furrowed brow, his large apologetic and trusting eyes, his still half-laughing dimple, and barks at the moon whose rays now pass through the bars and, from behind the base of his spine, light up the top of the tuft of his ass, mucked with blood. Having vomited and barked, he grows pale and collapses onto his side, spreads himself out on the dirt floor, legs open, member erect, throat rattling, as he trembles throughout his entire body, moans, and sobs the long, soft tears of a child; so is this how they get rid of those who disgust or frighten them: in subterranean cells? But I know enough to fear that his frenzy, if left untreated, might decline into madness; won't my barrack mates, sobered up, come and sit on the steps, before lights-out, to talk? And pass me through the bars what I need to sponge and clean our area?

Nothing but the officer of the guard, alcohol-breathed, pointing his flashlight at the corners, the wall, at me tugging the sawdust mattress toward the high point of the domed floor from which I have cleared, with both hands, the water mixed with the vomit of the kid now doubled up in a corner to finish expelling his filaments laced with blood.

I, who planned to exercise my memory by humming and then conducting pieces of my familiar music, now have to figure out how to sleep two to a narrow sawdust mattress and avoid having the army mate vomit on me; I also have to soothe him, calm his little howls: I kneel in front of him, begin to bark softly, echoing his high-pitched wails rasping through the vomit in his throat; my barks grow fainter, softer, more tender; his too, and toward the middle of the night, under the full moon, we fall asleep, each at an edge of the sawdust mattress, buttocks to buttocks, in the foul air that the predawn wind comes in to freshen; upon waking, all smeared with vomit from his forehead to his bare toes—they shoved him into my cell just as they found him, crouched like a wolf, digging the courtyard's sodden ground with his finger- and toenails—he thrusts his mouth toward the mug of sweetened coffee laced with bromide that one of the army mates from the watchtower brings to us—in the company of the officer of the guard, who is more accommodating than the one from last night—swallows the coffee, vomits again, but howls no more.

They make him disappear: a jeep starts off toward the division hospital. They take me to the water trough which the downpour has flooded; its blue-gray surface will be my only mirror for two months; but how to clean my prison cell? They roll a bundle of straw down the steps; they bring me down a sandbag from the camp perimeter: toward noon, when the heat, strong, has begun to dry out the dome of the floor, I scatter sand and straw in the vomit-filled channels: the vermin set to it.

I try to forget the reflection of my face: the sob I granted them devalues me, personally, but everything leads me to believe that the cause I am defending and bearing witness to, even in my awkwardness, is historically just: all that I have read, reread, of the initial conquest, cruel, of the repressions to keep it in place, the plunderings, the contempt for the history of the Other—for the historical consciousness of the "native"—on the part of France and, elsewhere, other colonial powers, the spectacle of the street, of postures, of gestures, the contrast between a dominant French language—even when corrupted in military orders and extremist bluster—and an Arab language, Berber language, made to seem inferior, pitiful and menacing, along with what I have seen in the villages and heard about the acts of violence committed upon a people subjected to terror from two sides, tormented by two senses of belonging, difficult to reconcile

—all of this confirms my faith in Algerian independence: the magnanimity of the Algerian people that distinguishes its torturers from the France and the French that it loves—we, the French, wouldn't be capable of a quarter of it.

On certain hotter nights, anxious about my notepad crammed behind a stone in the wall, I search for a more secure place, a crevice hardly visible even under the flashlight's beam; the insects scuttle between my fingers like words that escape me; worms writhe like written lines: Keep it all in my head? But I already have to keep there the pieces of music I reconstruct, themes, motifs, developments, variations, hummed or conducted standing, away from the barred opening: the short pieces from Robert Schumann's early years, before his marriage, the *Abegg Variations, Papillons, Allegro, Carnaval, Fantasiestücke, Kinderszenen, Arabeske*, I hum them, tap them out on the remains of a bottle rack; I sing to myself once more the five variations from the *Andante con moto* of Franz Schubert's *Death and the Maiden* quartet, so often hummed, sung, when my mother was alive, at school or else by two or three friends and me in nature, and the Eleventh Quartet, the *Serioso*, in its entirety; for *The Afternoon of a Faun*, for *The Rite of Spring*, for Beethoven's mysterious and "philosophical" Fourth Symphony, I have to stand up and almost dance; for Debussy's *Images* for solo piano, back to the bottle rack; when I think I have skipped a development, I start over from the beginning. My jaw hurts from chewing on all this music.

I do the same with the written word: the last scenes, in French translation, of *The Seagull* and *The Cherry Orchard*, in the Chekhov volume brought by a friend after my mother's death; I find them again, speak them aloud; The Young Captive by André Chenier—and its first line: "The budding shoot ripens, unharmed by the scythe"—The Chimeras, *Aurelia*, Kubla Khan and its first stanza, revived in *Citizen Kane*, whose deep-focus scenes I reconstruct for myself.

An army mate, having refused to take me to the water trough

under the command "shoot in case of attempted escape" underlined in red ink, is locked up with me a day and a night: in a very gentle voice that emerges from a powerful neck, he tells me of his apprenticeship at the butchery school, the instruments, the kinds of flesh, of cartilage, the bones, the entrails, the offal, where and with what force you have to strike with the blade, then, without pause, of the womanly charms of his "little mouse" whom he wants to make into his fiancée when he gets discharged; with his large blue eyes open forthright, he relates to me in detail, limb by limb, the furry zones, the radiant zones, the skin, how it covers the joints, the heart, how he sees it beating beneath, how he can keep his large gentle hand there for more than three slow songs on the dance-hall bench without dancing; he would like to let the hand descend lower but—he glances up at me; and when the blue begins to rise within the night, as he lies at my side, without looking at me, he describes to me the organ, its shape, its slit, its fur, how he plays with it, fingers, lips, tongue, teeth.

Independence

AT THE beginning of spring—sprouts of grass and little plants among the stones of the wall and in the cellar's hard-packed dirt where my sawdust mattress has begun to rot—I am transferred, on the pretext that the notes divulged by my interrogators from the Deuxième Bureau, together with my remarks and acts, might expose me, once freed, to reprisals from my wronged fellow soldiers, the most violent among us. I am sent through central Algeria, below the Mitidja Plain, with the barrel of an often-drunk regular army master sergeant's FM light machine gun pointed at me, in an unescorted jeep. Have my shoelaces and belt been returned to me? What do I have with me, if anything at all, of what's left of my things—papers, pamphlets, letters confiscated by military security, little objects of barter among soldiers? What's my little dog doing at this hour? No sooner does he arrive in my native village than he escapes into the mountains, grows feral there; from his jackal lineage he feeds on carrion, but from the hint of fox in his blood, he stalks the henhouses.

The spring dazzles me—I, who for two months in an underground prison was only able to grope at the packed earth, the walls, the sawdust mattress, in darkness more often than not, I would like to be able to touch these things that, furthermore, are new to me: the desert slopes rising toward the high plateaus, the red sand on bluish earth; amid the jostlings of the open-topped jeep, with the air of the journey entering my nostrils, my mouth, my ears, how can I keep in mind the anguish of my current condition?

I don't know anything about the place they are taking me to—how far from here and for how long (years even?), for what hard labor or prison?—Or even if they are taking me anywhere at all.

But I do know that I want independence for Algeria, happiness for its people, more and more firmly the farther we travel from the places of my humiliation; the driver Millet and the master sergeant stop to piss: the "old man"—hardly forty—worn out from his drinking bouts in Indochina, is slow to void his bladder, his FM machine gun jiggling at his shoulder; black gravel down below; the jeep idles in neutral; a temptation to escape—the same surge of excitement as in the dreams that arrive before sleep or dozing off by day: a thicket on the slope; what's below it? Forests, a gorge? A herd of goats? But to turn "traitor" and find myself alone in the cosmos, in military dress, my body still filled with doubt... Am I not expiating my arrogance here, along with other faults of former days? And how am I to free myself from my subjection to everything?

Of what use would I be to the other side?

Farther on, to our left, is that already the long and high Ouarsenis Massif? To our right, in the plain that spreads before us, the Chelif

River flows beyond the road and the Algiers–Oran railroad tracks where the Inox Express shines in the sun.

The barracks, where I am assigned a bottom bunk in the middle of a row of beds facing the windows, is set up in a low building at the camp entrance, near the company offices below the north blockhouse—in case of insurrection, everything is in place for suppressive measures.

My shoelaces and belt are returned to me, but no weapon. Windows, at last; and, beneath the blanket—useless in this heat—a sheet stitched up as a "meatsack." What did they do, over there, with my prison blanket? Burn it? Or will it serve again to haul quarters of pork delivered by the Supply Corps?

Collective life rather than isolation. And for my barrack mates, as I well know, the political grounds of my imprisonment are of little consequence, so long as I rebelled against the authorities, against the *croques*, as the conscripts call the regular army's commissioned officers and NCOs.

Almost everyone here is a convict, of a civilian or military court: some chose to enlist early to reduce their sentences in civilian prisons.

The barrack warden, whose bunk—his mosquito nets torn—is first on the left as one enters, under the first window: D., commando cap turned backward, agile hips—hops onto his bunk in a single leap, slick-faced; his eyes see what is human in others only for what can be tortured (unfortunate the prisoners in his hands, and how unfortunate to have been born cruel, and poor); cruelty is in all his parts: his voice, gestures, postures, his odor even, his breath; one sees his hands steeped in blood; his knuckles, fists clenched to strangle; his fingers cinching the garrote, knotting the noose, turning the bathtub faucets on and off, applying the electrodes; his crotch is the crotch of a man who pedals the "gégène," who commits rape; one sees his teeth severing the sinew or whatever else still holds the mutilated limb attached; his combat boots stomping on kidneys; his soles crushing faces; his sex parts seeking out the most innocent; his constant rictus, a remnant of the pleasure he takes in torturing; what is he being punished for? Crimes in the home country, or excessive cruelty in French North Africa?

The most taciturn soldier of the barracks, a Spaniard by birth, from Asturias, tall in stature, his adolescent face always held high and proud, killed his mother. The one who weeps at night in the mosquito net atop the bunk bed where I sleep on the bottom was convicted of a repeat offense of pimping, and is inconsolable for having shot and killed a stork: How, say soldiers more experienced than I, could he ever have seduced a woman with his tub of a face, his scrub-brush hair and his sniveling, unless he inherited a brothel concern from his mother and father, or has the right stuff in the right place?

To my right is B., the Place Saint-Lambert brawler, big, all askew, hovel-hued, tender eyes, skin, gestures; in civilian life a telegraph operator at the ministry of the interior, what could he be guilty of—orphaned, taken in by an ironing-maid neighbor, his little hands writing up his school assignments in the vapors of hot iron and cabbage?

To my left, V., the Guadeloupean, who blushes if you so much as speak to him: you can see the blood flowing to his pores; on his feet or seated on the straw mattress that faces my own where I lie reading, he watches me as he stitches and restitches his fatigues: when I glance up from my page at him, I meet his eyes, large and somber as if they were judging the characters who come forth from the lines and wanting to give them another destiny: it is said that he has killed.

The cruel one, at the back, tells the story of how he "brained" the shepherd and his beast, and makes the sound with his mouth and fists.

But at night I rise out of bed to peer at a large gecko cupped to a corner of the ceiling—in the cellar during the last days there were only the worms and, despite the daily or twice-weekly washing at the water trough under watch with loaded rifle, the maggots that fell from the vault and burrowed beneath my toenails as I slept. He must feel at ease with me, to lick his transparent eyelids so with his tongue, and he gives me the sense that I am once again a human being, or even speaks this to me, when, as he descends a little down the wall, I bring my ear close to his belly, which beats so many times faster than those of the sleeping soldiers, saying that I was right, that I am allowed to be right; I step among the soldiers' breaths: the little chains across their necks with the metal tags—our numbers for quick identification in case of dismemberment or burning—tinkle a little when the bodies toss in dream: their nudity lays bare the trembling, the naked nakedness of those whom the Law has bruised, threatened, afflicted.

I, my doubt subsiding; they, condemned, cast out, young—what could be said of me, if I were too feeble in emotion to feel compassion for others who, from excess of emotion, kill?... Here, in the slight, wayward pre-morning wind passing through the cast-open windows, they lie equal, good and cruel, in dreams where, as in earliest infancy, the being is governed by the force of its own truth, under the palm of God, refuge of murderers.

An owl shrieks from the conifer beside the blockhouse: I see it pass through the brilliance of the moon and swoop down upon its prey on the ground; what other thing, inanimate, could it feed itself upon without perishing, and its little ones too?

Some fellow soldiers, two or three years older than I because of the deferment that I refused, are quartered in the courtyard outbuildings. Having been informed of my presence by one of their own from the company offices, they come after dinner the following day to fetch me from the barracks and violate the order prohibiting me from mixing with the younger soldiers of my class, 60-2 A, quartered in the courtyard of the old farm where the company set up camp not long ago: they come out from their barrack rooms arranged in the stables, the woodsheds, and the other toolhouses and small barns; it's so hot that some of them even carry their cots out onto the pitted ground of the courtyard, and, holding their mirrors in the long twilight, prepare to wash up for bed—as if, in night and dream, they had to appear beautiful for their fiancées, their "little mouse," or their mothers. Amid the stale stench of the old cow dung, the courtyard smells of soap and more. With Ph., P., and M.—nonviolent, a political transfer like me, but here of long date and admitted to the courtyard—we speak in hushed voices of architecture, agronomy, geology, hydraulics, self-rule. No sooner has the evening redness gone dark upon the mountains beyond the river than the morning redness begins to light.

M. and I and other "politicals" will have to submit each week to a dictation exercise conducted by a senior officer who comes especially for this from Orléansville: followed by questions whose written answers he will use to judge the progress of our dangerousness, or otherwise.

First days: hard labor; am I allowed to attend the raising of the flag at reveille? But, with the movement of history accelerated and things heating up on the ground, the rules are suspended: we can even, under the protection of a dilapidated watchtower, go down to swim and do laundry in the river, among women, mules, horses, donkeys, herons, and partly wear our civilian clothes again. Commissioned and noncommissioned officers survive amid uncertainty, forced to handle us with more precaution, themselves weary of a war won on the battlefield but lost on the political front; here, on soil that will soon cease to be part of the Republic—we can feel, beneath our feet, this slipping of an old national territory out from under the new one—they stand torn between a far-off supreme authority; a temporary Algerian authority reputed to be corrupt; a contested Force Locale; a people in solidarity with its resistance fighters but already beginning to have doubts about its divided future governors—revolution or democracy? A National Liberation Army at once powerful and politically on the defensive; auxiliary troops liable to turn against their officers to efface the memory of their prior loyalty to the French;

and a contingent of army conscripts still loyal to the government of the French Republic.

I am summoned to the offices; it's to give me a package, forwarded by my former company, which a dear family that has come to replace my own has mailed to me: already opened, its contents scattered about on the sublieutenant's table; I have to give him an explanation of each object—does he write fiction too?—a little "Jesus" sausage from Haute-Loire, a belated wool sweater—will I have to spend another winter in the army?—a pipe, and a book of Faulkner's, *The Mansion*, recently published: What's this Faulkner about? From what I know of the history of French and European colonization, the violent conquest, the plundered and the profiteers, the small and large estates, the urban and rural servitude, the bonds between the subjugated and their masters, and from what I know of Faulkner, having read *The Unvanquished* and a little of *Absalom, Absalom!* I prepare myself to speak of the "South." But at the sound of the sublieutenant's *pied-noir* accent, I refrain from replying, for fear that the evocation of a people vanquished for its inextinguishable sin might lead him to believe I am thinking of his own people, and cause him to denounce me as an agitator again: sensation of my idiocy here, how I feel inferior to whoever bears stripes and corrupts in shouted commands our language, which I have now begun to reject along with the territory that is its host. What authority, except divine, could make me bow my head now? Not even the authority of French history which, here, a portion of the officers are dishonoring and causing to be dishonored. So I come back to the little "Jesus" from Yssingeaux—but not for too long, or he might confiscate it and eat it.

Even though I am prohibited from approaching any signal machine whatsoever, I begin reading the book in Ph.'s radio room: to the sound of his guitar, which I transform into that of a Southern banjo, I read the opening pages—I'll have to wait for my uncertain liberation in

November to see what it is in the original language, how it sings and moves and takes on color...! Mink Snopes, the trial, the return to his murder of Jack Houston, the motives: the cow; the fenceposts.

An illumination: I must create an oeuvre of the beast, of the idiot who speaks, of "nothing"; still a little more French psychological fiction, with "characters"—it's in the 4x4 command car that I wrote, a few months ago, while waiting for the battalion commander, the prologue to a book that will be published two years later—and then, soon, the epic of the idiot: through the idiot, destroy humanism, comprehend the political monster, the monster of the camps (culture didn't prevent the most vile dehumanization): an oeuvre of the fixed idea: What's Antigone after all, what's Electra...? Christ himself... the more the mind and its preoccupations are limited, the more the word is beautiful and ample: the fixed idea as a piercing and shattering apart of the real.

Clamor, disturbances, around the camp, lone figures passing restlessly, dark with the sun, with wandering, with hunger, with heat; it's of their ruminations that I'll make my future poetry.

In mid-June, part of the company is assigned to lay barbed wire around the summit of a nearby jebel where a sophisticated Franco-Algerian radio-television station is to remain in place... Is it in the Dahra Range, where Pélissier, future Duc de Malakoff, gave the order to smoke out the unvanquished tribes, a war crime "denounced" at Les Chambres by the son of Marshal Ney and by the Catholic Montalembert, after having been first "deplored" by Prime Minister Soult? Or is it nearer, on the mountain of El Aneb? I keep in memory the Ubu-abominations from the letters of Saint-Arnaud, future henchman of the coup of December 2, 1851, to his lady admirers in Faubourg Saint-Germain: "I left a vast fire in my wake; all of the villages, approximately two hundred, were set aflame, all the gardens pillaged, the olive trees hacked down...I passed with sword in hand [...] My own little Palatinate [...] Ah, war! War!" All the regimes of nineteenth-century France are steeped in the blood of the conquest of Algeria, last bequest of the eldest branch of the House of Bourbon.

For fifteen days, with leather and thick canvas gloves, we unload trucks, roll, unroll big bales of new barbed wire: we dig holes for the posts that we drive into the earth—resting on what beneath?—with sledgehammers. Down below, the ripening wheat flattens and unflattens at the passage of helicopters: soon to be harvested and packed into peaceful bales; birds of prey wheel and cry above us, as above future carcasses: Mink lifts and plants his last post in Jack Houston's field.

At daybreak, dew on the barbed wire; at midday, heated metal: the points pierce our gloves; our fingers swell, fester inside the gloves.

Where are we quartered? In tents? In "Churchill barracks" halfway down the mountain or at its base? Where do we eat? From permanent or field kitchens? And what? Wild game everywhere but we have orders not to shoot—and who among us still has his weapon? Artillery within the perimeter fence protects the worksite: watchtower, weapon stations, etc., which could just as easily fire on us if we escaped. Down below, beautiful colonial villages, fragrant sleepy shade beneath the trees; but these are times of high alert: villas, farms, eucalyptus trees, bougainvilleas, irrigation channels, public and private fountains; properties already abandoned; "indigenous" families are already moving into the manor houses and outbuildings, into the horse stables even (such is their beauty compared to the huts of mud and corrugated metal): tattered children in the halls; woodwork, tiles, living rooms already partly pillaged; cries of discovery and objects breaking, liquids spilling, wines, perfumes, zoological specimen jars; the most modest objects are the first to be picked out and taken; the more precious ones are for later—and not for them but for others, the new rulers.

One evening, in the slow twilight, we walk back up to camp from a small bar, along a sloped channel where the red-and-black water carries the day's rose petals; to the right, on the hillside, beyond a caravan camp of Rewels washing themselves and juggling with their monkeys, is a large villa, white and rose; we continue on among the abandoned massifs; from a lean-to beneath a eucalyptus tree, a little chant, neither French nor Arabic, reaches our ears: a girl, very pale, draws herself up, naked, within a black cast-iron bathtub; a little child, dark, plays among a tangle of rose, mauve, beige shawls: blood on the girl or mother's shoulder: it can't be from the deep-red setting sun; rifle shots down below.

Open air, work whose advance we can see: and so we measure the distance in days separating us from our liberty, but mine is uncertain.

In the evenings, with my swollen fingers upon the pages, I advance through the prison labor of Mink whose fingers worked cotton for thirty-eight years. How well I understand him. Mink to the judge: "Dont bother me now…" I envy him his sense of his right as a human, the right not to be humiliated more than he deserves, the right to exist, the right to go on, neither proud nor humble, to advance, to breathe, as much as the others; he helps me to find the sense of my own right again, which all the authorities—or at least those who do not understand that I am "other"—have denied me so far.

We write up the "*Père Cent*" that marks that we are a hundred days away from "*quille*," the day of our freedom: it's a double sheet, written in the style of a parish bulletin, which is the principal literary reference for many of us, together with what we call "books," the film photonovels we wipe ourselves with; among other features, each of us, with our consent, is given a nickname; thus our fellow soldier F., a tall, blond Alsatian highly attentive to his sex appeal, is given the name "Baby Soap Bal Musette"; for me, it's "Mes Prisons," after the book by Silvio Pellico. We receive the roneographed product the same day that I receive in the mail the one from my army mates in Greater Kabylia, along with a note and my nickname, "Brass-Eater," and the signature of everyone in the camp, with the exception of the beauty in his retailored uniform, who is better suited, they say, to cutting off the ears of those he kills—but doesn't he retailor his deeds just as he retailors his fatigues, tight against his beautiful form?

On the eve of the July 1 vote, against the bunk beds where they are packing their little bundles—gifts for their children, cigarettes, and wages—we try to convince two fellow soldiers from the Algerian auxiliary troops—whose service histories are unknown to us—not to go up to the douar to vote; the elder of the two, forty years old, father of a family, his scalp afflicted with alopecia, the younger one, shorter, curly-haired, bespectacled, sole provider for a very numerous household: these two men, who hadn't been of much concern to us—they are older, and of an unesteemed military status—suddenly become dear to us, and we to them: impossible to hold them back; they want to fulfill their "civic duty"; also, they want to see their children; standing before the elder, I can hardly detach my eyes from his jugular that swells when he speaks, light specks of froth at his mouth.

Gunfire in the jebel toward the sea: in the evening, we learn that they were tortured and had their throats slit.

Nights of July 1 and July 2: influx of villagers with large terror-stricken eyes, women, children, old men, rushing toward our barbed-wire-protected walls; a woman holds a bloodied turban in her outstretched hand, cries "Baba!"; children slip through the barbed wire, climb and jump into our midst; the radio commands, spoken orders confirmed by Morse code, which Ph. conveys to the captain, are to repel all attempts at entry: independence has been voted for, recognized, and proclaimed; we are on foreign soil—and what if these are throat-slitters, weapons-thieves? For two nights—commissioned officers and NCOs sleep or keep watch, locked inside—our hearts pounding, we find or improvise passageways and hiding places for the least able-bodied of those seeking refuge: the horizontal pit-galleries beneath the courtyard, the heaps of waste, piles of farm machinery; at dawn, our arm muscles burn from having tugged, tried to lift, and lifted the firm and infirm bodies, our bellies against the walls, the skin of our arms soaked in slobber, vomit, chewing tobacco, henna. We have to laugh to reassure them, to reassure ourselves—the children help us with it—but softly.

The line of the road that runs along the railroad tracks in the far darkness, facing us, at the foot of the Ouarsenis Mountains: we fear that it will begin to move with civilians or soldiers advancing to take revenge.

The owl keeps up its shrieking in the lulls of sound, but its hunting grounds are filled with human beings fleeing their actual or feared pursuers.

What authority are we living under now? That of France has ceased; that of the Provisional Executive of Algeria, established in April under President Abderrahmane Farès and his Force Locale—many young Algerians left our ranks to enlist in it—must surely now be superseded by the authority of the National Liberation Army and the Provisional Government of the Algerian Republic, itself divided into factions.

In the blockhouses, will our fellow soldiers on watch hold steady? A terror-stricken face sooner triggers a soldier to fire than to lower the barrel of the weapon before which the person advances covered in even thicker sweat.

Distant clamor of massacres, along the hollows: the sound rises; and, up above, clamor of massacres on the mountain peaks, crown of tears, of cries, like an offering to what gods? High plateaus of atrocities.

July 5, independence celebrations in Orléansville: we go there, the four of us, dressed half in civvies and half in uniform, hitchhiking; the driver of the truck is transporting the inhabitants of a douar, all dressed in white; in their joy, they clasp us in their arms, reach into their gandouras and take out photographs of children who they tell us will no longer have to go up to fight in the Resistance and who will live in a happy Algeria. The women follow behind, packed into a bus, its perfumes wafting side to side at the curves. Once there, lungs elated, I photograph the parades of combatants, children, little girls. We, anti-France at the time, anti-West, anti-nation, here we are in the seventh heaven of a new nation giving birth to itself before us, against us, with us.

Upon returning to the camp—gunfire in the mountains, to the north, to the south—we find the officers' quarters lit up but locked: They who conquered their enemy by force, do they see themselves as having been betrayed once again by the politicians, the diplomats? Do they regret having remained loyal to the legal authorities when those authorities now forbid them to come to the rescue of those whom it was their mission to teach to defend France?

Has the guard been reinforced around the armory? What commands are crackling in the radio room?

From inside the camp, at noon and at night, we try to catch the scent, close by—across the road and across the river—of the wheat already high and golden: of blood, of beasts in hiding there, of wanted men, hunted too.

Will the wheat all around be harvested? The large irrigation channels scrubbed clean?

In Oran, after a crowd panic—provoked or spontaneous?—nearly two thousand Europeans—many having come down from the villages to embark for France—are massacred, some of them flayed alive, hung from slaughterhouse hooks.

The evening of July 7, on the radio, Ph. picks up a Spanish station that announces the death of William Faulkner on the 6th; at the low end of the courtyard toward the river, away from the pits, we hold an all-soldiers dinner—cots carried outside with mosquito nets afloat—in honor of the liberation of one of us, an apprentice butcher, hot-blooded, who receives, at the same time as his release papers, a "scribble" from his fiancée leaving him for another man: heat, giant salad of cucumbers and merguez—but to our teeth it feels as if it's made of human flesh, such is the clamor that reaches us, from all around and from the hazy mountains, of the individual and collective settlings of scores. And we tell our fellow soldiers of what an "Old Moster"—as Mink calls his God of Justice who doesn't punish at random—the world has just lost.

I have my *Mansion* in a large, deep pocket of my fatigues against my leg; I take it out:

"Read to us, Pierrot... read the book!"

The brothel, of course, but it's too long—Miss Reba, the whoremistress—and we and they so starved for girls and liable to be shocked. Better to read the end, suited to this time of hate, of joy, good for some and bad for others, a time of wariness, of shame and terror for many, for those up there in cages soon to be tortured, bound to each other and waiting to be beaten, broken, brayed, maimed, eyes put out, skinned alive, scalded, roasted and returned to the earth as ashes or scraps without recognizable form or hue or smell—but are we of an age to "forgive," or to think "a man does what he can," or to think the thought of death and the weariness of living and defying?

And, without rising from the bench, as Ph. faintly plucks the blues on the strings of his guitar, I say:

"This is Mink, down in Mississippi; thirteen years ago, in 1949, he got out of the penitentiary after thirty-eight years; he goes back home to kill his cousin Flem who abandoned him during his trial; he kills him, goes back to his old ground, lies down in it..." And I begin to read, with difficulty, but in a breath of freedom, such has our language, over the past two years, under our subjection, reduced itself to so little. And yet I keep apart from this mass grave my mother's corpse entombed in France, in me:

"... into the ground already full of the folks that had the trouble but were free now, so that it was just the ground and the dirt that had to bother and worry and anguish with the passions and hopes and skeers, the justice and the injustice and the griefs, leaving the folks themselves easy now, all mixed and jumbled up comfortable and easy so wouldn't nobody even know or even care who was which any more, himself among them, equal to any, good as any, brave as any, being inextricable from, anonymous with all of them: the beautiful, the splendid, the proud..."

Exodus

THE SOLDIERS, lying on heaps—some with their shorts undone for who knows what girl to come flying to their organs hot as furnaces—warm their weary limbs in the already reddened sun. A light wind comes through corridors of vegetation bearing the scent of the sea, stronger here on the African coast, up from the great masses of underwater flora and fauna, the wrecked ships (of wood, iron, bronze, steel, silver, gold three thousand years old for certain); on the other coast is freedom, responsibility regained, its fullness, flesh, sinews, muscles, bones, organs, still growing limbs, mind, heart, weariness impossible, hunger for life, unconstrained, spaces to move through, intimacy, knowledge; and a little farther on, beyond Europe, beyond the West, beyond the native tongue, waits death unthinkable to us or heroic; immunity of the body.

Fatigues and green sweater, sandals, bush hat at my belt.

In the distance, inland, I see a partly underground passageway against the barbed wire and wall, through ripples of hot air, remnants of the autumn heat wave. I walk to it with an army mate. For the past three months I've been writing his "scribbles" for him, love letters to his home-country "little mouse," even down to the address on the envelope. Whenever I stray from the stock phrases customary among the conscripts and pen some more specific avowals—his tooth—he stops me short. I'd like to finally see a little of this forbidden land in which we live in servitude. The passageway descends, the walls of red earth grow narrow, damp bushes close in above us, a bird's song falls silent—shore bird or land bird? Disoriented by the gunshots? The clamor, the blows, the cries? From what little we know of the chaos now taking place within reach of our voices…

My hair, grown abundant again since they shaved it off in prison—why have they allowed me to grow it out longer than regulation here? They don't dare touch a hair on the head of this contingent whose obedience to the Republic has spared them another coup d'état—gets tangled in the thorny branches. My army mate curbs his panting—which turns to froth at his protruding canine tooth—comes back, helps me untangle what my father used to grab when I was a child, saying "How black it is!" as he embraced me. Return to him conquered, never! But love him more. And, like Absalom, catch my hair on a branch during my final escape—but what did I want from him—beyond him, beyond his beloved smell, tobacco, medicine, tools for childbirth, the smell of others, of peasants, beasts, woods, among which the smell of our mother, once mingled, has vanished, everything is now open defiance, everything must be so, for everything.

The fellow soldiers, from their half-drunken dozing—beer, bromide-tainted wine—call out to us to come back within the perimeter.

I bend beneath a bramble, the dog tag slips from the neck of my sweater, swings and knocks against the remains of a barrier across the passageway; my army mate, between his big spoiled teeth: "... the fell'rs, in ops, they hold it tight!" A burst of gunfire, toward the sea; who's killing whom? Birds take flight above, their shadows pass over us; the passageway deepens, and it's as though the brush and walls were closing behind us like the waters of the Red Sea upon Pharaoh, but the air is so gentle, warmed all day then cooled, so fragrant, so heavy with tears, torture, birth, joy, exile—so near, the steamships are loading.

He—who since the independence, and the nearer he comes to his return to responsibility and the exclusive embrace of his "mouse," has ceased his refrain, "I fuck even the goats"—reaches out his fists; his canine tooth presses against his lip (how many girls' red lips has he wounded, among the girls he says he's thrilled): "I don't mean t' bore you, Pierrot, but I smell woman!" Why does he call me by my first name instead of "La Classe," our customary nickname for others of the same draft year?

Does he already know something about the place we're heading toward? Has he taken advantage of my desire to see "the real thing, civilian life"—even in a state of war—so he can "go on the prowl" under the pretense of exploration? What difference does it make: his reasons are as good as mine, so muddled.

Will the passageway, damper and damper, rise back up to the surface? Our soles hit mud: in war, civil war, everything is suspect, from ground to mountaintop; this black mud, isn't it blood? This passageway, a place where the hunt for human prey comes to its end, a place of slaughter, struggle, throat-slitting? Mines? Have our Op Zone engineer-corps soldiers' eyes forgotten so quickly? These coagulations, these slivers that hang from the brushwood, aren't they scraps of dried brain?

Pieces of Barbary fig limbs in long heaps ahead of us, their rotting fruit covered in flies, thorns untouched: Should we walk over them to continue on? Won't this premature act, of pure desire—which I could postpone until I'm free—jeopardize my chances of being freed at the legal term of my conscription?

My army mate, who has only been reprimanded for a few drunken escapades, attempted public intercourse with dogs male and female, goats male and female, military charges for excess of no political consequence—he has no reason to fear he will see his service time extended; the army looks after the socially deficient; with me, they have a score to settle; I am seen as an inward mental accomplice of the Rebellion, of its subversiveness, its massacres, its victory, of the army's dishonor, the exile of the French of Algeria, the loss of the empire. Stay tense and expect the worst: how I've lived since childhood.

But the din of a European feast—religious?—beyond the heap, the row of eucalyptus trees whose scent thickens in the pre-setting sun, the buildings with their gleaming-red rooftop terraces, draws us on, causes us to climb the droning, unsteady heap, walk upon it, step across its thorny parts: Have we passed beyond the perimeter? Are we still within it, the barbed wire far ahead of us?

My army mate—with the bottoms of his retailored fatigues rasping against each other, sheltered, an instant, from the din—gropes about for something in his hip pocket: his member, already? Small coins for the children? For a drink? His fat fingers—at noon, dark meat, Hénaff pâté at four p.m.—pull out a little all-plastic mirror that he lifts to his sweating face as he walks; with the fingers of his other hand—ring finger missing: not enough for an exemption?—he combs his mop of hair, grown out again on him as well, sleeks back the strands, plasters a few against his temples; the protruding tooth, what to do with it? A charm in fiction, but in immediate fact?

As the bushes open out, the din increases; a noise of motors, backfiring exhaust pipes; the trench where an odor of putrefaction holds me back, though commonplace in this tragic territory: rubbish heaps in heat waves, presumed mass graves, unknown carcasses from threefold civil war. A road, freshly paved—the persistence of administration—public, which means we're beyond the military perimeter, in sovereign

Algerian territory—how are we adapting ourselves, since July 5, to this transformation beneath our feet?

Cross over or turn back? On the other side of the pavement, clumps of dry or burnt shrubs; beyond them music, carnival voices, rasps of microphones, an overamplified choir of little girls; between the clumps, farther on, entryways of ocher-colored buildings... Nothing to the left except the glare of the sun; nothing to the right except an already darkened mist fallen from the quick-departing day—toward Algiers.

In five weeks, if I am released, this world beyond the still steaming pavement will be mine, ours, but beyond the sea then, beyond war, in quieted home country, with its immediate destiny assured, friends from before, new friends from the army mates here, streets, squares, celebrations, cinemas, books, children, girls, sheets, beds, glasses, entirely civilian clothes, free to come and go, shoulder unburdened of rifle, head unburdened of helmet, no identity papers except those of a citizen, go out at dawn, come in at dawn—winter will have almost arrived—the Louvre, the bridges, writing...

Cross over and, me at least, risk forfeiting this dream? Wait longer: and at the moment of the liberation, if the authorities keep me back, my army mates will stand together to demand my rights.

Since, suddenly, with his shoe-sole on the asphalt, he hesitates, thumps his belly and even trembles a bit—his cheeks puffed out—I advance, heart quieted now, step from one firm spot to another, leap into the ditch where, beneath the dry dirt, something spongy crawls with maggots. He, behind, blows at the swarms of flies that target his fat head, his never-closed mouth, his stump of a finger, his stewed crotch.

A concrete path and here we are, among bougainvilleas, in front of the first building of what appears to be a housing complex for French military personnel. Children, parents, would they report us? Rust in the hair on our head, in our body hair, in the folds of our fatigues, in our nostrils, our ears, under our nails: in the company camp and then in Algiers, barehanded, loading and unloading heavy equipment since August.

A ball falls and rolls to my feet: for me, afflicted with severe myopia since age eleven, balls are hostile objects that approach half-unseen, that, launched at head level, can strike eyeglasses, break them, turn me into an animal down on all fours against the ground; but here it's an object from civilian life; I kick a shot and feel reintegrated in advance. The ball soars, falls again, disappears into a thicket. A song, whose melody I recognize, despite my listening having been reduced to my transistor radio's choppy music for the past two years: a chorale from the time of Claude Goudimel, close to the Protestant hymn I sang as a Catholic child.

Where is the singing coming from? My army mate, thumping his belly again, sniffs an odor of grilled meat (odor of bodies dry-burnt to cinders) in the pine-fragrant air; we keep silent. On one side—to the left—choral song, ritual, little girls, gentleness, reconciliation, lemonade perhaps... On the other side, meat, men, women? Of what allegiance? Wine—unadulterated with bromide?

I'm hungry too, I'm always hungry, but eat, here, in civilian territory? Civilian, "freedom" food? Make things worse for us? And what if it's some belated Organisation Armée Secrète sympathizers? The remnants of the uniforms we're still wearing would be enough for them to cast us out... or worse. If they are liberals, separatists, or even resistance fighters returned to civilian life, here we are, here I am... but what political offense could they accuse us of: nobody is anybody's enemy now.

My army mate stamps and blows at the furious swarms. We walk around the building at the base of which dogs whip through debris, food waste; at the sight of us, they scurry off: Our fatigues, our belts? A bone still fleshed with meat, too big to be that of a human or medium-sized beast, blocks the path toward the remains of a villa, truncated columns, shattered fauns, bowers, cracked basins, the space opens onto a dried-up lawn, a long facade where flowering branches take root and intertwine—but of what color in the dazzlement of the end of the day? Is this a dream? If so then we're still slumbering, he and I—how would I know if he's dreaming the same as me or I the same as him?—side by side with the others and within regulation? The scent of roasted meat has vanished; did it rise to our nostrils out of the ruminations of our hunger?

From a large arched bay window on the ground floor, the sound of a guitar and then of a small drum reaches our ears; my army mate sniffs at the heat emanating from the window, paned with a stained-glass colonial scene at the top: "I smell woman, I tell you!" his voice strangled; it's that his throat is finally forming words other than the ones we all pronounce, our common language, where, for the past two years, a dozen or so expressions, such as "we ain't out of the woods yet," have sufficed for our condition of servitude and reinforced it; have been suitable for all situations, whether concrete, abstract, particular, general, the physical mingled with the emotional, only inflected high or low, fast or slow, clear or throaty: Has being out on an adventure in civilian life made him go limp? He, so bold in his attempts at mating, blushes as he rubs his fly with his palm.

I am not familiar with his member; the fur of the dogs he mounts conceals it from our sight, his fists in the shower too.

This villa, even in its dilapidated state, probably intimidates him, peasant that he is, like a manor house—he would be more apt to stand in front of it, cap in hand, request in mind.

Behind the windowpane, pale forms, raised voices, laughter warbling from pursuits or embracings. Game room of the family residence—spared from the eleventh-hour housing speculators?

Turn back? A sound of gunshots toward the coast, repeated toward the interior; the lower slopes of East Algiers? Revenge killings? Interrupted lootings? Belated drills of the young Algerian Army? End of hunting season—prohibited during the war? From the direction of the buildings, snatches of song, the "Kassaman"—anthem of the Algerian insurrection, still banned in the very first days of July, when I used to listen to it in the watchtower, headphones hooked to my Sonolor, a song that confirmed me, French as I am, in my right to wish for the Algerian independence: the truth-power of music, even war music.

The dog that has followed us since the asphalt where he yapped at the swarms of flies, weary of gnawing at his bone—of what beast?—rises on his hind legs against the glass door, scratches at it. The forms grow agitated; a sound of things being put away, of bodies brushing against each other, the door half opens—have looters taken apart the latch and made off with it? We step back, to the side.

Crushed barbed wire, ditch, pavement, path, buildings, and now an answered door... our fate could change here; knives, axes, hooks are at work throughout the territory; and our throats are still fresh. The light reddens, the shadows hasten over the groves, the rocks... a bosom pokes forth, half out of its camisole, a shoulder bare beneath the strap, a cheek, a profile; eyelashes blink, a mouth half opens, nostrils flare, a scent of fresh shampoo, a hand descends between a pair of thighs, against light shorts: dangerous days, everything that can be cut, gouged, slashed, tugged out from inside the body, beaten, cut to pieces, ripped, burnt, must be defended.

The face turns toward us, toward the setting sun; the chest breathes: all the girls that we have seen, glimpsed, heard, smelled, wished for during the past months now gather themselves in her, so near, breath to breath, in reach of our hands, feet, mouths, ears, nostrils, skin to skin, bone to bone, heart to heart.

She speaks, her teeth sparkle, her nipples, beneath, peep forth as well; her radiant hand—soiled with, heavy with what?—begins to rub again; my army mate has retreated; over my shoulder I see him trot between the building fronts and palm trees, toward the east corner of the villa. A zizzing between the half-covered breasts: Flies? Bees? She, with her pink-nailed thumb, shakes the edge of the camisole, the frill: What is it that flies from the shadowy hollow and alights upon a nipple?

What is she saying, hurriedly, French mixed with Arabic—but is she speaking? Isn't it me who makes her speak within me?—she steps back, opens the door wide upon the half-darkness: between the camisole and the shorts, skin pink and tawny, pale vermilion, and the navel like a shell flush with the surface of water or sand: I see the buttock, the small of the back, the haunches; it's indeed through a throat, through half-open lips, that she "speaks," softer and softer now that I've seen almost all of her: my palm wants her haunches—not uncovered enough for me to see them—my lips her mouth, my tongue her tongue, my teeth—which I am not familiar with—her teeth which she, at each mirror, looks upon, lips curled back; my heart her heart. The rest of my body is a confused, indistinct upswell, an accelerated blossoming, sap, branches, stems, trunk; my palm, my lips, my teeth, my nostrils, my brow, my cheeks, her nape—so pale, despite the sun, the sea-bathing, more delicate, more luminous than Sophie's, which was already grown plump, flabby, coarse—just barely a touch of light-auburn down, the little bones lying flush at the surface not to evoke the skeleton but rather for fingers to play upon; fine tight-curled hairs take root there, as if blossoming from her scented soap; the dog shakes itself and leaps into the half-darkness where the little drum has ceased but fingers still dampen its sound and drag upon it.

A girl, at last, a woman to touch without having to speak—and speak in a zone of civil war where a single word can mark you as the enemy; nothing but movement, gesture, let nerves and muscles do as they will; but couldn't such a radiant bosom, having kept its radiance under harshest sun, contain a word set free, an intertwining of verbal delights waiting to rise, uncoil, and come out from above; mute from too much to say?

Mute from the war? Bomb or massacre? Rape? All infirmity disarms me, leaves me helpless to my heart, I go toward it as a brother. All of a sudden, the present is impossible, abolished, everything that anchors a person—pleasure, happiness—forgotten, and only what follows, the afterward, the consequence: coupling, escape, pursuit, wanderings, offspring, death without death.

Into the half-darkness, where now, her hand in mine—what a release throughout my whole body—I follow her whose bath-scent grows stronger, and within this scent another odor, and I hear a brief clicking at her ears—coral earrings? My lips advance toward the top of her hair, my other hand rises toward her hip in motion beneath the flower-print rayon tight against it; just a hint of a worry about the remnants of rust behind my ears, inside my nostrils: Would she smell it before putting her lips, tongue there?

My so rapid heart, why have you ceased to pound my blood so heavily I turn pale and falter? The member must have taken it all for itself: Think no more of it, think no more of any part of me, body, past life, life itself, let only my member live... thought, keep away from there! My member, outpace the thought, go before!

Here, in these times, there are no couplings other than rapes... no approaches, no play of hands, nor anything else that composes the daily routines of love among those who are the same age as I but foreign to me now in that forgetful home country, only concerned with the return to school, the season's new offering of books, the autumn sessions of parliament and trade.

A climbing rope sways at what seems the center of the large room, hanging from a fat ring on the ceiling where my eyes can make out painted coffers; swarms of flies circle round it, knocked by the thick plaiting but returning to it.

Toward the far end of the large room where the light filters through torn blinds, a form, a body, of the same age, and dressed almost the same, but dark-skinned and without breasts, stands with the little drum against its groin: a boy—I don't think to look between his thighs—has he dressed up in the girl's spare clothes? An earring of hers at his ear? A bracelet of hers at his wrist? Barefoot too, a large crate beside him, and upon it a plate from which his long hand thrusts aside the muzzle of the dog that growls at me and rages at the zizzing flies; he stands still, turns his face toward the half-dark: Is it my fatigues? The string of the bush hat at my neck? For him who seems to have an eye for clothes, my green sweater—homemade—isn't enough to put him at ease. His mouth wrinkles up the same as his brow. The girl's pale, fresh arm comes from the half-dark; I have to take its opened hand in mine; between the wafts of roasted meat from the plate that clatters at the dog's muzzle, I catch the scent of something raw but beginning to putrefy: A half- or uncooked part of the meat still warm in the well of the plate adorned with flowers?

The hand pulls me to the side; the thumb, fresh, presses against the little bandage I still have in the hollow of my own—a wound from the barbed wire that we cut, stretched, and planted in El Aneb in June; from her companion's throat, which pulses even beyond speech or swallowing, comes a succession of high, gravelly, hesitant, irregular fragments of Arabic and Spanish words: Distress, disapproval, threats?

In his other fist, he kneads at a scrap of bluish wool on which I see dried streaks of red: in the half-darkness, the creases in the shorts of the girl who's leading me stain dark; her mouth curls back as if for a broad kiss, her teeth translucent ...

A pre-sunset gust of wind stirs the canvas of the deck chairs stored away at the back on the mosaic tiling, sets rocking a horse of white and gold; the girl's haunches do a horseback rider's to-and-fro; her breasts spill over the frilled edge; vertigo seizes me with sweat; I force back, to the emptiest part of my mind, the temptation to let myself be pulled toward nonexistence, toward my vanishing from the world. Focus all my senses, one by one then all at once, on the plate of meat, on dead things first—with something alive it would all begin again; that which allowed me to overcome the arrest, the interrogations, the months in the cell, could, at this moment, so close to freedom, cause me to lose my sanity—and whoever loses it once, will lose it again ... Force all my senses toward this pitiful piece of what was once an animal proud or gentle, toward the infamy of meat-eating that everything in me condemns, and keep my sanity—which only those who've never risked losing it would have us believe isn't worth keeping.

The girl's throat emits a kind of gargling; her hand tucks one of her breasts back into her camisole, catches in midair the scrap of wool the boy tosses her.

Noise of debris trampled underfoot along the opposite facade of the villa, the inland side: Could it be my army mate trying to enter the house by a servants' entrance—better suited to him? Once inside, would he take the girl more boldly, more bodily, ruin her for me? Her halo of fresh warmth, her fragile story, still so vague and yet so certain: Would he, with his voice or his protuberant tooth, sever the thread that binds her to all the most secret things I have dreamed of since early childhood: the half-beast, half-human state in which to escape all constraint, all ordinary obligation, my merely human self?

Noise upstairs: How many stories? Wood floors? Tiling? From a shattered window comes the thickened odor of putrid rawness; but from the girl's shorts that move as she moves, drawing me into deeper shadow, the scent of the dark stain that spreads from crease to crease covers the other odor that, together with the odor of garbage, can be smelled in everything that is spoken here, printed here: blood, for the most part innocent blood—but blood attracts blood, one gets drunk on its smell.

The girl turns her chest now, moving toward the darkness again, her haunches arched, her hand still holding mine; with the other she wipes the blood advancing down her thigh: For how long? Is it only blood? What other thing might come from a girl so beautiful, so free without speech? What fluids, humors, poisons, potions?

She, so merry, he so...Who's the one losing blood?

The horse begins to rock again, a ray of light through the creaking door reveals the face of a red-and-white Pierrot lying with its ruff against the wall atop a pile of multicolored tent-cloth, garlands, paper lanterns, croquet equipment, large picture books—of fairy tales, geography?—framed reproductions.

Hold the hand of one who with the other is wiping blood from the place that is still forbidden to me?

Undo all that binds me, military status, surveillance, evidence of submission, threads of my deliverance, and so, at last, wild, know a woman?

But what is it she wants from me that makes the boy grind his teeth as the top of his hand, thickly veined, touches the flat of the drum—what did he pull the scrap of wool out of? His pocket, his partly open shorts? The notch of his chest? Is it the same piece as before?

Now she throws it back at his bare feet; the dog yaps at it, lays his claws upon it, sniffs it.

Outside, through the door-window swiveled back against the wall, in sudden silence—cessation of hostilities, gathering thunderstorm, general suspension of the horror of History?—the singing of the little girls rises firm: verse, refrain, resistance, resolution, faith.

If only we had gone that way instead: gentleness at last, confidence in the Good, scents, perfumes of religion, of its objects, even if less abundant here—Protestants—bouquets, prepuberty, a respectable place if we are taken by surprise and recaptured, instead of here, in a pillaged house, with open flesh in reach of our hands and mouths and members, a dog, menstrual blood, belly-rumblings, strangers, desire, whose for whom? Accessory to vagrancy, to looting, even to rape...

Her hand clasps mine again; my entire body, aching from head to heel, shivers from it, the first hand of a girl I've held in twenty-four months, except in dream: but it's been so long since I even shook a boy's hand—except during my two leaves, old friends, new friends. Army mates and officers salute each other. The extreme, constant lack of privacy—never alone except in the watchtower: not even in the shitter—has abolished the handshake.

Will I have to speak? Even if the poverty of our soldier-idiom has diminished my stuttering, how to respond in time and aptly, even with these two whose capacity for speech is destroyed; even if my stuttering brings me closer to them—as to all infirmities—more certainly than all the lectures and parables taught to me in childhood.

The staircase, short, rises into thicker darkness like descending into a cellar: its steps are covered in real marble; do I have the right to set my foot upon them? Everything that bears a semblance of officialness, of legality, of law, of hierarchy, is now forbidden to me, including this marble on which, with one of her hands tightly closed on mine and the other still occupied in her shorts, she steps and steps again with her bare feet more like fingers, heels upraised—if she lowers them it's that she want us to stop and... for what she wants, it would be best for me that it be done wherever it's done, and not on some ordinary prop, common, a bed, a sofa...

But what does she want, with her breasts spilling forth and shining, vermilion, in the shadows, a scent of motherhood already rising from her when, from below, between her thighs, to the faint sound of the rubbed hairs, an odor rises, impossible to place, between sea flesh and fresh dung at best? Me, my army mate too, we've emerged from underneath the jets whose war machinery we clean; twenty-two months of communal life, servitude, nights in "meatsacks," nights on watchtowers in all weather, vehicles leapt into and out of, worksites, training exercises, salutes, roll calls, two months underground for me in a prison cell, plus my three incarcerations in the home country, anguish, cunning, derision, youth—have all these finally given me a body?

Stuttering, bespectacled, carrying myself like a student without being one, deprived of the advantages, but I have scraps of joy, of spoken jest, pantomime, not to mention what the older girl from the "Sphynx" wanted to pull out from between my thighs and that she didn't even glance at, but only lifted her whole fresh open forthright face upward to look into my own, with a brief tinkle of laughter...

On the stairhead, in heavier shadow, I can make out a Spanish coffer with iron fittings, an antique copy? Unpillaged? What's within it? Does she know? And she too, what does her infirmity shut within her? An animal dashes between my legs, a cat, tail raised, between my calves? Above us, noise, footsteps, draggings. At the bottom of the short staircase, the boy now stands on the tips of his long bare feet in a pink ray of the un-set sun; the girl's breath quickens at her chest, one of whose fat nipples I can see stuck to the frill of the flower-print camisole; his hand holds the scrap of wool in the pocket of his nearly transparent short-shorts; the dog shoves its muzzle there—why didn't it snap up the meat from the plate? Does it prefer fresh blood to cooked flesh? A form laid out in two parts is beneath the folds at the edge of his thigh: between the thighs, nothing but a mound; his eyes shine almond-shaped beneath the painted lashes, sparse eyebrows under curly black strands, but between the delicate ribs, black hairs sprout—almost up to the neck.

She, turned around, with her hand upraised to chase him away, emits belly rumblings and makes foam with her lips; he steps backward toward the sun's full ray; she, with bared foot, stamps at the carpet, thick beneath my soles; he steps back again, beyond the ray, with the dog's muzzle fixed to his pocket.

She takes my hand again in hers, warmer, leads me, sure-footed, into the dark: we brush against furniture, edges of ottomans, backs of chairs, heavy vases, doors of open wardrobes; I can make out large paintings, frames I imagine to be gilded. I look at them closely, force my naked eye to perceive their colors, forms, flakes of paint perhaps, at last a little art, to touch. The cat raises its tail again to my knee; the girl takes my hand in hers again; I hear the rustle of fleece at the base of her belly and, by the faint gleam of a gilded object set on dark wood, I see her arch her hips again at the sound of the cat's mewing, a bit of folded flesh poking between shorts and blouse. The corridor—or is it merely a part of some great sitting room or something else; is this residence what it seems, or less private? My sandaled feet get the feel of carpet again—the corridor continues with no daylight ahead: to the left and right, stout-framed doors, what do they open into? No glimmer at their foot—closed windows, shutters? Paintings, engravings, on the walls; up above, vaguely, mounted ornaments of metal? Wood? Stucco? I bring my eyes close to the prints, my glasses in my hand, colored engravings? By the colors, and partly by the drawing they compose, I get to the center. A hunting scene? Horses, mythological figures? A large painting, gilded frame worked with floral motifs: ramparts, horses, shade of oriental trees, capitulation and submission of rebellious tribes, burnooses, bowed turbaned heads: on one side, kepis, epaulettes, gold braids, sabers poised on ground; on the other side, medals, treaty papers in victorious hands, rearing horses.

A buzzing: Flies upstairs? Swarms knock against objects on the wall but their direction is clear... The corpses, carcasses I dimly see at the back of the painting, in two heaps, to one side clothed, to the other half-naked. On the horizon, flames, and girls in tatters fleeing them... medals on slightly wrinkled tunics in the glorious foreground, heavy-jowled fools soon to be bedecked with honors at Tuileries Palace balls and in prefectures; orchards and harvests, pillaged.

The girl's hand tugs me farther on, toward the scent of a bath, but not as fresh as I would like; the daylight should return to us through the little steamed-up windows, brushed from outside by palm branches, on white or blue tiling, but there is still only the darkness faintly broken by the colors of the paintings, by her own nape and face when she turns to me with her little cooing laughter; will she tug me to the bath I long for and fear: as for her, how will she keep her slightly sullied face, eyelids, sockets, corners of the lips, nostrils even, which I see in this darkness better than I could by day because she breathes closer to me here, marked with little dots of gray dirt—like freckles on others—which the washing would erase, this dirt, this suint, these scratches she seems to revel in like Diana at the hunt? But, for me, a bath at last, in porcelain, but with water of what sort—poisoned, unmonitored (inspectors murdered), or tinged with blood? In this territory now shifting its foundation, its heart, its law? And, naked inside, clothes and belongings outside, with no defense, no recourse against the factions, or tracked down and found by the military authorities, all the more brutal now as they would be acting with permission in foreign territory, since France's extraterritorial jurisdiction has shriveled.

I hear her sniff at the air; is she still bleeding? The boy, is he still kept downstairs with the dog? The cat rubs against the base of my legs again but doesn't raise its tail this time; ears flattened: prey, close by? Above us, heavy forms are being dragged across the floor again—a terrace already, or an inhabited floor? The darkness shifts; to the right, a casement window budges; the blinds creak: the corridor has ended; by the more open air I can tell we've entered a larger room: beware then of furniture possibly spared from the plunderers, advance with hands and feet and knees out front; but she—whose nape with the lightest touch of down I can make out by the luster of her skin alone, unbent by any submission, but atop a back that I could see downstairs is slightly hunched, like that of a beast accustomed to searching the ground—steps forward freely, but with a sideways shuffle that releases the odor of her thighs, her creases, her armpits: at each press of her fingers against my knuckles, a high-pitched muttering stirs her nape, uncovers a part of her shoulder; her breasts, in front: Are they out, or has she tucked them back into her shirt?

How far, how long am I to let myself be led through darkness by the hand of a mute girl whose blood is becoming a familiar smell? Not a single mirror on the walls, not a mirror atop a piece of furniture to catch even a deflected ray of this seaside pre-sunset autumn light that will not last. Still a snarling of flies, toward the upper story.

But, before me, after a movement of the darkness—her shaken hair?— a gleam appears, cheeks and nostrils and lips now luminous from their flesh alone, from its fresh, firm depth; higher up, the two eyes, wide open, one grayer than the other, laughter in the iris; my heart hasn't beaten this hard since I was warned of my arrest in April—but it's when it beats the hardest, at risk of bursting, that my mind is clearest, firmest: the blood spurs it, feeds it.

Her lips move, curl back; I lower my eyes toward the opening of her shirt; the breasts push against the flower-print fabric; one pokes out on which I can see the tawny areola with its rose-blue nipple; she cradles it in her upturned palm; a part of her strong tongue slips between her teeth where the last of a sunray filtering through the blinds stirred by a gust of seawind marks the outline of a broken tooth amid the froth that rises from her throat.

A gust of wind again: a bird, tangled in the slats of the blinds, struggles in the darkness, long wings, puny feet; a swallow, its migration gone wrong, flings itself upward, hits something that rings out like a chandelier, steadies itself there, the wings flutter again, bird-droppings fall on us; little cries, wingbeats toward what might be a bust or a sculpture of an animal, group of animals, far beyond the girl whose breast is still caught in the blouse with its frill slightly darkened with food, with droolings of sleep and desire.

I hold my free arm back from trying to catch the bird, a childhood reflex I maintained among the paths, gardens, parks of Paris.

Is the swallow perched, crouched flat on a tray atop a cupboard? Inside a coupe glass? Has it let itself slip behind a painting tilted forward from the wall? Up close, would it smell of the terrestrial airspaces, the maritime airspaces, that it has flown through in flocks? By its scent, from the intact fragrances of its throat, its wings, could I guess anything about its nesting place? A barn in the Dauphiné, a seaside villa in Brittany? Its age? Look into its eye; the pleasure, long ago, of keeping my gaze fixed there, as in the eyes of cows, of the littlest animals, dragonflies, crickets, frogs, to find in them the token of our resemblance, our fraternity, our equality—their enchanted lives in air, in burrows, in bulrushes: that's for later, my deliverance into civilian life.

A rustling of the tuft between the thighs, a rolling of the breasts, foam at the lips, a small fluttering of wings; the bird stops to think—is its head moving in the darkness? (is this darkness to it?)—resists the pull of sleep (so many hours spent above the sea-swell, the waves, the spindrift)... let it fall asleep; has the girl heard the wingbeats, the collisions, the little cries? Have her nostrils perceived the scent of the bird; her skin the stirring of the air above us? Her fingers unlace themselves from mine; her palm opens on the threadbare wool of my sweater at the site of my heart, which races again: for so long, not a single hand on my heart, on my cheek; nothing but hands of men on my shoulder: Dare to lay my own on hers, two of whose fingers knead at the hole I have in the green wool; I'm wearing, beneath, the remains of a khaki undershirt stewed in rust and sweat—for us in the company, our undergarments dry in the wind on wires in front of the barracks, the same ones rewashed for months—is she looking for a hole there, to slip a finger in, its nail longer than those we used to see on the milk-bar girls, and curled? To touch my naked skin: shoulders weary, nape, I await her hand; breasts—how can they swell and harden for me like this—so near, and beneath a slightly forward belly whose innocent navel I saw when we were downstairs, there is that tangle of flesh, external, internal especially, of tufts, the picture of which, in a 1954–55 pornographic magazine I flipped through in secondary school, left me with the image of a little butcher's shop that only lacked a blade with which to deepen and redden it even more.

Shall I risk my member there, from whose erection, with the attendant desire of my whole being which it sustains unto its own extinction, I have pulled, since earliest adolescence, the rudiments of the figures, scenes, actions—the words, especially—of my future poetry? To yield to woman—though all my life I'll feel this lack, this humiliation—would make my heart grow tender, diminish its capacity, its duty of universal empathy, in favor of an individual love, whether consecrated or not—even if threaded with adjacent passions and their sterile dramas, prolonged in a lineage, with customs of mutual support that I want nothing of—how this would release the tension necessary for the spontaneously transgressive Great Work, and constrain me to writing well-mannered, moral, conventional fiction all my life, for my dependents. Each time I feel desire for a girl, a woman—desire for a boy, indistinct, immediately transmuted into desire for whorehouse figure, itself indistinct (anal penetration inconceivable)—this dilemma recurs, this temptation and refusal of the softening of my heart, my life, this choice between surrender and a stiffening, a standing straight—I'll have experience, later, of this arrangement, cruel (for both parties), misunderstood, mocked, but the need is still as strong today; I have in me an intact carnal desire for girls, for women; I can follow a plaited nape, a neckline filled with breasts, a domed and thoughtful brow, a pregnant belly, strands of hair beside an ear, a voice lifted in desire, a hand, a stroller: apparitions of a forbidden world—though "ours"—that the figures and voices of my fiction, still unfinished to this day, cause to vanish again.

Is she still bleeding? To bleed and desire: Even wild, wouldn't she burrow herself away until this unclean blood ran dry?

Her mouth—as her finger advances through a hole in my undershirt toward my chest made strong by heavy labor, toward my nipple—puckers again around the tip of her outstretched tongue; I don't see it, I guess it by her constricted breath, by the little sound of suction, by the swell of her breasts that nearly breathe upon me; on her arm I see a gleam, her neck, throbbing, the edge of her nape, her head turned back toward a creaking at the far end of the room, a footstep a little lower down in the darkness: a smaller staircase, from the game room? In a coupe, a bowl, atop a small cushion, in an open drawer, the swallow hops about, rises on its wings; my hand, which I cannot see, reaches for the little wingbeats; what does it touch instead? A crease, creases, a hip clasped in shorts, the curve of a buttock that straightens against my palm? I can see at last the eyes that should be shining... lashes blink over them, crusted at the tips—mascara, flows of tears, of wrath?

Keep my palm on this edge of a buttock, push my fingers farther forward; and if I'm able—by accident?—to touch the buttock, could I touch the breasts? And then, could I move my lips toward hers? For months now, they haven't touched anything but food and the fur or muzzle of some favored animal, chance mascot; lips forgotten, by me, by all of us, except for a few when they lick-kiss the envelope that holds the letter to their "little mouse."

Who is she? What age? Who feeds her? Who looks after her? Does she go outdoors? Who understands her mutterings? Whom does she understand? The boy, down below, a milk-sibling?

At the possible far end of the darkness, a staircase creaks; the finger on my chest stops short; the breath quickens; finger and hand descend the length of my hip, retake my finger and hand there, tug them. A faint red gleam—the more the night closes in, the more the light returns as if from the wooden floors, the walls behind the objects, the drapery, the tapestries whose fabric and colors I can sense as they quiver in the slight wind, exhaling scents of the far south—the gleam illuminates a narrower passage toward which she leads me; the scent of a bath, which I could already smell in the corridor, grows stronger; but, past the narrowing whose floor slightly descends, we cross into a room less vast than the one we left, where the girl's ear, before my own, perceives the sound of the swallow taking flight, the knock of its body and wings against the blinds, the fall to the windowsill, the flapping of wings, the muted cries... the cat dashes between my ankles; I force myself to like the odor that the girl gives off from her thighs, moving more and more rapidly: her breath, too, has a scent of fresh raw meat—who brings it here? From where? How does she eat it? From the plate? Out of her palm? Am I the one who—since her first apparition, fresh girl of an afternoon, in the entryway—has provoked her wildness as the conclusion approaches?

The flies, in little swarms, follow us beneath the ceiling above which footsteps move; the golden light touches a few floorboards, a disemboweled toy, a crushed plastic-stomached baby doll that stares at us with gouged-out eyes; she tramples it under her foot whose long-nailed toes also strike the bristle-backed cat, but it doesn't let go of its scrap of bird whose wings still flap; a woman's perfume approaches at our backs in the re-shut darkness; the girl's fingers, fresh, strong, tighten on mine, her mouth turned back toward mine exhales a sourness only smelled on rabid animals; at last a being who smells in all her parts, whose every movement makes an odor: the auricles of her ears smell of wax, her eyes, liquid, smell of certain roses that have to be lingered over a long time before slow long scent of paradise awakens (ecstatic gaze lifted toward Him who cannot be seen, the inconceivable), each of her breasts, each of her armpits...

The girl, breasts all tucked back in, lets go of my hand, darts her own toward the latch, turns it, pushes open the door; the light, pink, red, gold, dazzles us: long, wide, all tiled in white, with sinks inlaid in wood such as I've only seen in films, gilded faucets, two, three bathtubs, broad little frosted-glass windows with handles, big white hotel towels, some folded in piles, others hanging on the wall, still others crumpled and torn on the floor; she leads me inside, casts about with her eyes, one of which, I notice now, is shot through, beneath the slightly droopy eyelid, with a red streak that the setting sun causes to sparkle beneath the gray of the iris: all that I have at the base of my belly between my thighs, that cluster of flesh, member and parts—coiled as if it were another body beyond ennui (less susceptible than the mind to authority and programmed stultification, less alienable), which all of us possess, permanent, natural, in every circumstance, even during salutes, roll calls, drills, troop transport, work—now unroots itself from too much stiffening, carrying off with it entrails, heart... a darkening, an illumination; but she, who takes my hand again, does she see it, does she hear it? Trails of sand on the floor, sand at the bottom of one of the bathtubs whose raised gilded plug, touched by a ray of sunlight, is rimmed with red where flies walk upon it.

The woman's perfume is at the open door: a high-pitched muttering swells the throat of the girl whose mouth has closed again; her eyes and her hand, unclasped from mine, act quickly: a dazzling white drawer with a cut-glass knob lies open in a cabinet whose glare conceals its forms from me; she casts into it her hand, whose veins protrude at the back and fingers; the boy shakes, rages forth a few Arabic words that I can't understand, except for the saliva that froths at his tautened mouth, where red lipstick peels off in flakes, a small unopened pocketknife in his fist.

Me, soldier half in uniform, held on suspicion with release deferred, on private property in a foreign country that was only lately enemy territory, between a mute girl trying to defend herself and a boy-girl threatening her with a pocketknife, here I am, I, so hesitant with girls, placed in a position to defend one who wants another thing from me, against a boy who barely looks like one but doesn't want me to be desired by her: Desired? For my body? For the game of it? For what she can sense of my comprehending her brain—my nostrils almost able to smell it through her cranium, with its deficits, its excesses more fragrant, my fingertips almost able to feel the network of neurons there conducting decisions good and bad, step to the right or left?—and the boy doesn't want me to desire her either, as he can see I do, with his furious eyes, whose oiled gray kohl intensifies their humanimality; and despite or perhaps because we, she and I, are under threat, I desire her with every sinew, including the one that fails him: the blade is bared before the empty creases of his shorts so thin that I can see the crease of his thigh; because my heart pounds harder for her, as she leans toward the cabinet, breasts out, it pounds less in fear of his blade; then I see the scar, short and pink, that a premature little fold of woman's flesh had concealed beneath her chin: Could that be where he strikes? Or, not he, but another, others? Too deep and well defined to be the scratch of a cat...

So far, I've seen such a transparent garment on a boy only in the vaguest visions of my clandestine writings, interrupted two years ago; slightly loose at the hips, tight at the crotch—when and for what does she wear it?

Is his perfume hers, for after he's forced her to take a bath?

From a heap of instruments in the drawer—my father not so long ago used to reach for them with a steadier hand, and the sound is softer here, wooden handles, ivory, nacre, soft brushes, in my father's cabinet it was metal—she takes a long razor such as I've only seen at my paternal grandfather's and at the barber's; she opens it with one hand, takes my hand in the other, brandishes the razor in her fist, blade up; through rooms, corridors, comes a quicker and quicker trotting, a slipping of claws and paw-pads on parquet floors: The dog? Close by, a mewling, a hissing and spitting: But what would a dog want with a raw, mostly eaten swallow?

In a golden ray of the sun through a little window that a gust of wind has opened, the two blades shine and, beneath them, with its heavy odor of a male in rut, the dog, half-feral crossbreed, haunch already lowered, scrap of grilled meat in its fangs, eyes on the girl.

The danger makes me grab her shoulder, which she shakes free to steady her fist on the handle; she mutters and, withdrawing her hand from mine, advances it firmly, with index finger extended, toward the dog's muzzle; the dog tilts its head, whimpers, drops the piece of meat between the boy's ankles, turns its empty muzzle toward her crotch again, searches the fabric there; a swarm of flies slings toward the meat: the girl's throaty laughter makes the blood well up again in her shorts toward which my urgent hand was beginning to descend—to take, seize hold of this forbidden flesh and, later, look at it, examine it in detail, tame it, touch it with skin more naked than my hand: lips, tongue, then member—the face-to-face at last—since "that's how it's done"—and that's how, within me, my heart, spirit, future, confronted poetry.

My hand on her nape to lessen, stanch, this blood with stimulating palm? The one that sensualizes, soothes, heals, gives courage again.

My member is, now, her: a living thing, not muscle or text. Neither subjugated nor reduced to servitude—the "infinite servitude of woman" that, at the same time as figures of slavery (human bodies possessed by humans) enter irrevocably into my poetry, prohibits me from placing my hand on woman (the male member, on top, penetrating her as she "offers" herself below, to perpetuate that endless rape of the flesh on which life feeds); and that she might "take pleasure," might seek her pleasure from it, changes nothing: Did our mother groan with pleasure beneath our father as I heard her groan in the throes of death?... Hell-sound; we are all children of slaves, of servants, of those reduced to servitude.

Does the girl even have need of a pleasure other than that of playing, little piece of meat in her mouth, raw or cooked? Does she need to experience, mute—deaf? All her senses?—the penetration by a male, upright, as if in passing, to survive in this large villa and its approaches, the spaces of which I do not know?

The dog, collarless, large, gaunt, crossbreed of sheepdog and jackal like many of the dogs here, places his morsel at the girl's feet: For her to take her share and give him back the rest? Or for her to take it all? Will she bend down, reach her hand into the swarm? And me, how do I get out? At the little windows the gold shifts to red, palm fronds slip across the panes, the lemon-tree flower straightens itself, the human clamor begins again: cries, songs, barking dogs, strident birds, tires on rehardening tar, furniture smashed in hurried loadings; the singing of the little girls has stopped; is my army mate within these walls? Would the dog have barked at him? Could he have found some girl not horrified of his protruding tooth or willing to make the best of it? Or some stray female of an emaciated herd scattered from gorge or refuse heap by machine-gun fire?

But the boy—could he have drawn the knife only out of fear? Not because I might take her from him with my member, deprive him, but only because I am a soldier?—advances toward the girl who, piece of meat in her teeth, fly-swarm at her nostrils, steps back with open razor in her fist; the boy, keeping the pocketknife open, advances toward one of the bathtubs, turns on one of its tall gilded taps; the coils of the water heater blaze above him; he touches the thread of water, advances toward the girl; she, brandishing the razor, meat on the floor beneath her foot, squeezes herself, still tugging me by the hand, into a nook beneath the little windows; here I am before her, between the brandished razor and the open pocketknife; the dog searches beneath her foot.

Up above, beyond the brilliant white ceiling—on a terrace?—the dragging begins again: the flies, above us, reinforced by the swarm from the meat, follow the dragging.

On one of the long glass shelves above one of the sinks is an inclined photo frame: behind the glass now fogging up again, a very young couple seated, she with her hair loosened, a baby on her knees; he in soldier's uniform, his hand upon her bared shoulder.

The boy, whose woman's perfume has intensified with sweat, steps forward again; the water flows, already warm; the dog pulls at the piece of meat beneath the girl's heel; her foot crooks back in defense, but touches the boy who puts the pocketknife away where it shows through beneath the creases of his pocket; his mouth utters a few words in which I recognize Berber, gently guttural, and French: "*bain*"; his hip shakes against my front, I step aside, the girl whimpers, high-pitched; her mouth curls back, her brow furrows again: A reproach? The boy, a little slobber between his spoiled teeth, eyelashes blinking upon a slightly clouded eye—can he see from this side?—he brings his long hand near the furry wrist of the girl who, with a kind of caterwaul, turns the razor in a sunray where little winged insects bestir themselves at last in full light.

The dog, meat between its fangs, places itself at my side against one of the other bathtubs, empty but suddenly giving off a musty reek of fresh decay—human? Could the terrace, pipes, sewers all be filled with carcasses? Ages, factions, species mixed together? (How much time has passed from downstairs to here? Dream time?) Is the rope, downstairs, still swaying? Does the blood in its strands, this menstrual blood, dry faster than blood of war?

The dog gnaws at the piece of meat on the tiles; the boy grabs the girl's hand, keeping clear of the open razor; the dog lets go of the meat and growls; the flies scatter; from beneath the filling bathtub, a cockroach, then two, then more, scurry toward the flies; the boy pulls away his hand; the dog takes up the meat again, toys with it between his fangs as he might do with a bone, watches me; at my right shoulder I feel the weight of the weapon strap, my USM1 rifle I haven't been allowed to carry since my arrest. The girl, breasts out and quivering, haunch raised again toward the dusty corner, brandishes the razor again; the boy, pocketknife in hand, repeats in a lower tone the words that come from his jaws; since the dog returns to his piece of meat, growling with his muzzle to the ground, I tell myself he must have seen this act before and thinks no more of it than of a game that only the addition of the girl's menses might escalate; the blades cross, touch lightly; will I have time to wash out the blood that my fly and crotch picked up from the rope? Let it dry and scrub it at camp? The blood that I should have picked up from her, my curves bare-skinned against her groin, the embrace deferred as we moved through the dark ... if it has to be done, then it might as well be done with a girl animally indisposed, throw all my strength into it, all my weakness kept mute in my brain. Three hearts beating, a bathroom echo, is the water still running?

A single movement of my sole on the tile—but resolute—stops the hand of the boy, who steps back, knife open; I advance toward the girl who has lowered her fist and lays her blade against her shorts, slips it between her thighs as if to wipe it clean; the boy closes his pocketknife, stirs the pinkish water, turns around, seizes the girl's shoulder, rubs his jaw against hers as she huffs amid the steam of the hot bath, gasps, her breasts tucked back into her camisole, leans her head over the water; I follow the dog, who trots, limps, toward the door; I turn around; the boy selects a block of soap from the three arranged on the rim, turns it beneath the nostrils of the girl who looks at her reflection in the water, mutters; at the base of her raised haunch, I see blood, crimson, at the top of the buttocks that she wiggles and shakes, at the seam of her shorts.

The dog pushes its scrap of meat beneath the bathtub among the cockroaches, slips its haunch underneath, picks up the meat again, shakes itself, pushes open the door, barks in the hallway, its haunch bristling: the cat again, with the swallow between its teeth—what separates them from human plunderers dividing among themselves the meager remains of the massacred, or from scientists and scholars claiming and protecting each of their discoveries? In my view, not much, and yet at the time I still believe, a little, in that God of humanity alone.

Distracted by a hooting that rises through the garden and draws me near the little windows, I let her take my hand in hers, familiar, whose calloused palm tickles my own; a sunray lights the dome between her downy temple and her ear hemmed with hair, a lockbox of sounds to set free—the secrets of her wildness, murder, abandonment, the words shouted in her presence that made her mute? Her nipples, beneath her round chin and its little fold of fat, have poked from the frill again; I see them harden, their pink darken, sweat in the steam. The boy, who now holds her by the neck, sees me looking at them, the saliva flowing to my lips for them, and, lower, the front of my army jacket moving; he wrinkles his mouth, nostrils, brow; but his furry-wristed hand descends along her shoulders, her back, her haunch; a long, pink-nailed finger lightly touches the spot of blood, the curve of the buttocks: how beautiful she is from both angles: in profile, her face, beyond the sun's ray, is more gently luminous, more radiant, than all my rose-white entrails passing from hot to cold. Despite her anger, purer still, her eyebrows, lashes, the rise of her lips, the curls of her hair, hardly a trace of it: the back of the soul laid bare—pleasure?

The nail scratches at the seam; the girl stirs the water with her plump hand beneath the steam that smells of the sea: His words, jaw to jaw, does she understand them by their vibrations? That she has to undress, that he will help her—could she have lived fully clothed since the event?—Should I leave? See, see again at last that tufted groin through which I have to pass, with my faithful member—my single oar in the subterranean lake of Hades, pass through woman, by woman, to live again.

And if she enters the bath, sits in it, lies in it, and if he gently lathers her whole body—the blood, will it have ceased?

Does she have to? Or could she keep her filth, her crusts, her tangled hair and tufts, her stains, her streaks, her smears, keep herself ready to run away, in her odor of all things that makes her untrackable—even by dogs? To live for a time with beasts wild and tame, with fugitives, or from hand to hand; but hasn't she led me from downstairs to upstairs, then into the darkness, to this bathtub, so that I could see her step into it and wash herself there—and so that I could bathe here naked with her, rest my body here, weary of dismantling, lifting, hauling, loading, heaving, since the middle of summer? If not for the bath, then for what other purpose? What other room? What space surrounds the rooms, the hallways through which she led me by the hand? Are we alone here? Is there a room, farther on, colder, with acrid scents, muffled sounds, where people are dying—where people are writhing in agony? Alone? She, alone? Surrounded by her kin? Armed guards at the door? Shutters closed against exodus?

The boy reaches for a brush on the blue rim; his palm knocks a flask whose stopper isn't sufficiently sunk, the scent rises through the steam to my nostrils, half-clogged with blood ever since a bridge component plunged into them while we were unloading cargo in the port of Algiers; a pang runs through my heart: How many dramas of childhood and adolescence were enacted, long ago, in our narrow bathroom shared by the seven of us, facing full south onto the steeple and the dark mountain . . . and She, my mother, "my Darling" already—whom I dared to call by that name, far from my father—in the scene that never ceases of my inner voices, ancestors, descendants, kin, saints, artists, kings, executioners, God the Father, God the son, who speak to each other, defend each other—wrath, reconciliation, tears—and die, with last words . . .

Washed, perfumed again, clothes fresh, does the boy only want to wash her hair and groin, the parts of her most susceptible to infection? But she, her mouth puffing toward me with parts of human words, animal cries, sounds of objects, sounds of Nature, her hands clutching the flared edge of the bathtub, she draws in her neck, sticks it out again, stiffened, beneath the hand of the boy who lowers it toward the stream of water from which she pulls away her splashed head; already he scrubs her face with soap, but will he, as if carrying out an assigned task, soap her wrist, arm, naked shoulder? He quivers with trembling: Does it put him in a rage to wash the wildness out of this milk-sibling to whom his inferior birth—an embrace, a penetration, perhaps, from before her mutilation, or something else that I still don't know—causes him to be enslaved and bound until his death?

She shakes her head, pushes the thick soap away with her shut mouth, opens it again to bite the boy's forearm, holds him with her teeth, but he tightens his fist around the soap: blood flows from his elbow as the girl unclenches her jaws. I can see her heart beating beneath the camisole stuck to her chest by the splashes and the boy's heart, beating faster beneath his prominent ribs: Would they tear each other's hearts to pieces? Her eyes on the little chain at my neck, her teeth ascending along the links, descending, nibbling at my identification tag…

In the hallway, the living lay hold of the corpses.

Outside, in the distance, a bugle plays the motif under which we live, and which a few of us, with thick voices in camp beds, transform into the rhythms of Saturday-night dances in the home country.

I advance through the hallway, the cat scurries off, the dog pushes at my ankles with his muzzle, meat all swallowed; the frosted-glass bathroom door shuts in a gust of wind. Through a window held partly open by its hasp, I can see the middle of a fire escape; two men slide a large burlap bag down the iron staircase beneath the flies: Objects? Bodies? But as the bag slides it leaves a trace along the metal; the flies set to it. Stepping back behind the window frame, I see their dark heads turn once and turn again: Municipal workers? Police? Looters? Murderers?

The bugle plays its motif again. Return to the girl? Where has my army mate gone? A chandelier above me clinks its prisms and crystals: the bugle, again; will I return home without having done the thing I know, which would make me completely a man, as it should? I don't have the heart; I hold on to the window frame: so near, the organ one must penetrate with one's own, let it be swallowed there, persuade the girl, a being, from within: not only with lips at her ear, hands, voice, my heat, my muscles, but also with that muscle of which History and the Patriarchs are made, within her entrails; until now, I've had that muscle only for my art, for its clandestine portion only; should I change my lineage, if all penetration produces fetuses—and she, what could she know of the precautions that clean girls take—exchange vague figures, of indefinite sex, for real children?

Is my army mate dallying over a docile dog, a stray goat at the city limits? Does the bugle remind him that he's forgotten we crossed the camp perimeter by mutual agreement? That he promised me we'd return to camp the two of us together—we swore it upon his tooth.

At the window, the swarm plunges. Cold—winter soon, snow on the heights, on the remains of the war, mass graves, persecutions, exodus—a shiver seizes my shoulders: Where, on what girl or woman, did I first see that organ, the one that humanity comes out of and male pleasure enters into—how many more times will couples still couple beneath their nightshirts, unseeing? Eyelids closed?

Every sexual thing that I experience with a partner I forget, or else it's as if I hadn't seen anything: the scenes of my clandestine writing, in their vagueness itself, are stronger (negative-positive); and so it is that I remember what I've written more than what I've done. Each time is the first time.

To enter into the girl would be to bind her to me for life; and do I have the right, me in possession of my senses, to take pleasure, to confirm that I am male, in that body with its mutilated mind? But her beauty… couldn't it restore the wholeness of her now troubled reason? Am I not a little mutilated myself?

At my feet, the dog vomits its piece of meat: Could this be the smell of vagina turned inside out?

In the bathroom, the water has stopped running; grunts answer words like rocks in saliva between the jaws; has he grabbed her hair? The scent of its twisting reaches my nostrils; their jawbones clink against each other; the clinking changes into an odor of enamel knocked and cracked: every gleam, every sound changes into scent; every odor into color, into forms; a machine gun fires in the far distance: finger on trigger, the brain of the killer (decision), the heart of the killed, the mother's cry.

The flies blacken the steps, on rot, the sun reddens: How will our army mates in the camp conceal our absence at evening roll call?

Sounds of splashing, soapy water flows forth beneath the door: Has he undressed her, his fingers trembling on hems, buttons, slits, seams, creases, and has he made her step across the rim, blood drying at the top of her tufted thighs, organ opened, downy hairs at the back of her groin? Will she come out through the doorway again, all washed, dressed in fresh clothes—a spare set in the drawer—or in scraps of soiled fabric against her scoured skin?

Soldier, able to protect them, even as a foreigner now, but male, endowed—officially certified: the doctor of the "three days" draft physical exam confirmed to me that it was so—I can see why the boy might want me near the two of them, or far. She, back within his smell—has she forgotten me? Does her organ, beneath his fingers, open for me? I hear a sob, a moan; the dog lifts his muzzle from my foot: his calm makes me think that this is usual; I want to rest on time itself, lean against it, and for it to stand still before it continues on, and I as well; the darkness grows luminous with the setting sun; I advance, the dog nips at my heels; at the far end of the ascending wood-floored passageway, a gold-and-white-paneled door budges; a bedroom appears, an unmade bed, a wall covered with scenes in red and blue; among the folds of the sheet that has slipped to the floor, remains of toys, bashed-in baby dolls, mechanisms on rickety little wheels, torn picture books: other children, gone or silent; I advance farther on, but the dog whimpers: on the wall, little scenes from the classical age, modified pinup figures, cowboys in colored crayon, carriages converted into automobiles, malicious turbaned figures, tips of parasols sharpened into cutlasses, banners repainted in the red, white, and blue tricolor, or green with red crescent, rivulets carrying ruddy water under little bridges; an odor of fresh bodies? Nothing but musty effluvium: Are the children already at sea in ships' cabins bound for the home country? Fleeing toward the ports? In limousines, toward the border? Or worse. The dog sniffs at the toys among the folds, lets out a whine and yelps; his muzzle rises back up along and under a fold, reaches inside the sheet, lifts it: flies heaped on a streak of red... fingermarks; higher, a dried flow of blood: Could it be from one of the bodies that the two men outside are now hauling through a side gate whose bell tinkles at the entrance to the small park, to carry them off in tarps toward a vehicle or cart? But on the floor no trace of blood or footprints—could all the blood of the body (slit throat?) have poured out into the thickness of the mattress? The dog doesn't sniff beneath the bed frame: Was the body put into its tarp atop the bed?

I move slightly, reach my hand toward a light switch; the displacement of the air carries a brief stench of animal decay to my nostrils: Could the switch be booby-trapped? I pull back my fingers; on the wall, the faint light of evening now touches only the hand-drawn additions in crayon; the old centuries disappear among the lines and colors of a contemporary hand; what hand—youth's? Adult's? Of victim? Of murderer?—traced these wild strokes, these stark colors? When? Why? This blood on the sheet—is it from the same hand, or from the murderer's?

The blood of war: as with sex, each time is the first time; the blood of peace: the blood my father would bring back on his fingers from his doctor's office downstairs to have lunch or dinner with us or, more often, after us; the blood that would spurt from the wounded or infected flesh that he cleaned and cut with his scalpel as we, my brothers and sisters and I, children and adolescents, helped him to hold down the patient, child, adult, or aged.

For us children, in times of peace: the taste of blood before its smell, of our own blood, first, on thumb or tongue or lips, then on a knee, but the smell of child's blood is less strong than the smell of adult blood, later, in crime or war.

For the child of peasants or peasant-workers, animal blood can spurt or flow as familiarly as a spring or stream: birthing of dogs and cats, bovine births, calving in barns, lambing in sheds—the death of the pig after the pursuit and catch, the slitting of the throat, the bleeding out into a bucket, fowl cut to pieces after the fatal twisting of the neck, throats of ducks, geese, turkeys, slashed, game from forest, field, or wetland, shot, blood in convulsions on the ground, stuffed into game bags, pulled out, bleeding with wild blood nearly black, flung onto the broad communal farmhouse table.

Since earliest childhood, that remnant of blood shining at the edge of the asphalt, from which my mother averted my eyes, her hand on my neck: June 1944, the blood of one or all of the young Forces Françaises de l'Intérieur shot dead by the Germans during their retreat toward Paris, the blood of war.

No sooner does it appear than it is carried off into thought, in all its darkness or fullness of light, heaven or hell (purgatory is moderation, anti-art . . .), each time it appears is like the first time—as with love, longing: every curve of the face, of the body of the beloved, every inflection of the voice, every bend of limb, every odor, scent...

Each manifestation of the real is merely a precursor to or aftermath of a continuous thought of the violence of the world—the violence of life—of human against human, of nature (disease) against human, of human against animal, of animal against human, of animals among themselves, of the body against the spirit, of the spirit against the body... a confirmation of what I experience, imagine, continuously and in silence.

I live almost everything as if at the edge of reason. In the interval between reason and its explosion.

Or at the edge of losing consciousness, in the case of texts, for as I read the slightest phrase rendering the account of an atrocity, I live it from within those who live it and, in addition, from the perspective of one who watches it take place: penal torture, political torture, "the miseries of war"; and the more drab the phrase, the stronger the emotion which is more than emotion, the hallucination (thus, in the work that I make, I have always oscillated between distance and immediacy: between the spectator—the witness forbidden to cry out—and the tortured). For a long time, as a child, I could not reopen the page in the *History of the Girondists* where they are at pains to properly decapitate the fugitive from the vineyard, tracked down, seized, judged, condemned, brought to the scaffold, lest I faint for real, my half-decapitated head lolling upon the desk, or the pages in *The Toilers of the Sea* where Gilliatt, clasped round by the tentacles, senses that the octopus is about to swallow him whole (his member clutched and pulled toward the beak)—here as spectator, God letting his self-devouring Creation do its will—lest a tentacle dart out from beneath the bed and clasp me and crush me or some close relative or friend in the vicinity, and all day long this tentacle would "gird my loins," as it is written in the Bible, and as I made it my custom to do to myself and to my brothel figures.

Between two gusts of seawind, a few wisps of the singing of the little girls, with boys' voices mixing in as if to trouble them.

Machine-gun fire, ahead, toward the coast, behind, toward the outskirts crammed with peasants displaced to the town's resettlement camps. The bathroom door opens, rosy steam in the still dark corridor; the boy and then the girl come out, hand in hand: they peer into the room that I have entered; he lets go of her hand and leaps in front of me, smooths the sheet out again with hairy fist, but she, only her face and hair washed, crouches down, threshes the toys in a fold that remains on the wooden floor; with the back of her shorts opened upon the base of her haunch; undulations of the little bones; breasts, fuller than before, beneath her still sudsy tresses; perfume above, odor below; her eyes watch me above a handful of toys that she starts to lick with her short flower-pink tongue, perfect of form and flesh, even though I imagine she darts it into every dubious or dangerous interstice, into swarms of stinging insects, over every blade, from little knives to cleavers, to saws; what sounds, what sound, reaches within this ear so finely hemmed, with its auricle traversed by the halo of a rose-gold sunray? Below, over the floor, does her organ open as she crouches, is it still seeping blood? The flies—grown sluggish in the darkening light and beginning to return into holes—drone heavily around her.

With a swing of his buttocks against mine, the boy knocks me from the scene, takes the girl's hand again, lifts her, muttering, to her feet: the pocketknife, closed in his nearly transparent pocket, would he take it out again and open it if I brought my fingers near these breasts that in daylight would dazzle me: Make love, here? Her contours turning the scent of their large fruit, forbidden but visible to all from afar, ripening in nature, capturing all light, all temperatures, this outgrowth of more tender, more ephemeral flesh, how is it attached to the bust, to the firm flesh (as one speaks of "firm ground") between her bones, rooted in her but capable of being detached from her like those of Saint Agnes? Made for hand and palm, above, below, the nipple made for the mouth; in the palm, alive with separate life, but attached to History...

... like the breasts that Gauguin's Tahitian woman cradles in her platter of red flowers in the first painting by a master that I ever saw (not counting the one of a peasant and his little girl in a red kerchief hurrying from one low thatched cottage to another, of the Polish Romantic school, framed against the Tatra Mountains wall hanging in our home) when I was thirteen and a half, in summer, at the Musée des Beaux-Arts de Lyon, my hand in the hand of my mother, who had traveled with me by bus from our town on the edge of the Rhône piedmont to the city, for a radiation session: What is the other Tahitian woman on the right looking at, with one breast bared at the edge of the blue swath that rises to her shoulder? Or rather, what is she saying to the one beside her? Our hands clasped each other more tightly; that yellow breast with its blood-pink nipple tied in blue cloth, wasn't it—did she know?—my member and its uncovered glans, already tied, deliberately, in the tug and release of the tattered cloth that I would cut out for myself from the scraps of fabric in her stock of sewing material and then sully with coal or motor grease before I put it on and strung, unstrung, strung it again still tighter against my "parts," to the point of making myself a girl's groin by flattening them or, on the contrary—with the fabric closely hugging the form of the swelling parts—the loincloth of the crucified Christ and the soldiers, spears upraised all the way to the hem-scar of the circumcision—not so much to make myself orgasm (already desire was impetus, creative force; and orgasm, the standing still of time, a "bourgeois" satisfaction) but rather, though I did not yet know to what end, in order to impel what I had begun to draw-write in secret, under the cover of minor poetry, issuing at first from Romanticism and later from Symbolism, and minor open-air painting: to cause to appear, through the upswell of desire (desire for what body, back then, for American-style pinup girls in tight two-piece bathing suits, for girls and women in paintings, forsaken, contorted, pursued, dragged? Desire for desire itself? To escape from the ordinary?), new words upon the page, perhaps, fragments of words, tempting and more. Words that drew me toward the future. Words that, by accelerating desire, produced, at the same time as the explosion—the spurt of reproductive fluid, countered by my imagination—a secretion that, like the secretions of Christ, in agony, then mocked, then nailed, manifested to the world the intensity, the truth of the commitment, the writing, the flow of ink, the indelible trace, for me at least, in the eyes of God, which is to say in my conscience, of the sound-vision of the "brothel," which very word made me stiff, even before I was able to place within it figures that I would have been hard put to summon up cold: there had to be an act, a risk, since the spurt was followed by a time of depression, very long for me as a child, during which I had to overcome, with my feeble solitary strength, the temptation to end it all.

My mother's hand unclasped itself from mine when our father picked us up at the museum steps to take us home by car, and to take back from me my mother, so weary and not able to say it before me in a still more tender embrace.

But, during the whole trip home, along the Rhône, undammed back then, tumultuous, I made the three breasts of the two Tahitian women—the third, belonging to the woman of whom only one is visible, I saw fondled by the large, fleshy hand of a half-naked Tahitian man whose caress perhaps evokes her smile in the painting—appear in the writing that I would take up again that night, as soon as everyone was asleep, in my room under the eaves, made them disappear amid the throng of men, forms of Art exhibited here in the sole desire for gratification, for selling, reselling, in the outlines of a market where I carried out only basic calculations (prices of bodies, prices of acts) whose numbers called up more intense desire than their translation into letters: art, in this outline of a society, was mocked and sullied, paintings and poetry desecrated like Christ and his martyrs, whom, the next morning, in my broad-daylight writing, sketches of regular poetry, I would uphold as forms of saintliness, order, concord, fertility, purity...

To force my hands not to touch the breasts, I fix my eyes on the flare of the shorts—but what is my vision, my sight? At the top of my being, of my body, I no longer perceive anything except what I have between my thighs, confused, upthrust like a volcanic blister, an idea in radiant expansion of which the final formulation would be the erection of the member—mind, heart, past, future, universal matter, assembled for...? A hand coming out of the sun?

These eyes, these globes, their roots, lodged in the eye sockets of a skull that no one would ever think to look at, hardly even at that of other living things, winged or temporarily rejected: of a head formed of flesh and covered in hair, whose every feature I forget, mouth included, when I speak (to live, forget your body); it is from within a ghost that we live: at most we see the hands, the feet, the knees when we sit.

Take off my glasses to reduce the rejection of the other? But what would I see then? From a ghost of me, the rest, a ghost.

Keeping them on, I see the flare of the girl's shorts shake lightly with her small laughter—has she seen, with sight heightened by deafness, the effect of my desire upon the greasy hem of my fatigues? Or, at her nostrils, caught the scent of my fingers drawing back from the radiance of gentle sleep and milk on her half-bared chest? From the touch of noble breasts—touch the mother... at the risk of smelling a fecal odor rise from the flare, I give free rein to my nostrils, let my sense of smell do what it will: it is not an odor of dried excrement that rises, but rather the odor I smelled downstairs, the odor that the army mates attempt to describe, lying on cots, film photonovels in their lifted fists, all speaking at once, with animal and alimentary analogies, always the same, day after day, week after week, month after month, with explanatory notes and biographical context unvarying—a collection of testimonies in which the visual, tactile, olfactory, and gustatory experience of the female organ, as described by the hotel bellhop—prostituted, though not aware of having been, to old, rich women with tired sex parts—and by the sailor—familiar with schoolteachers at vocational schools, brothels along the banks of canals—predominate over others of Saturday-night dances, of village benches at night, of cars or truck cabs. The odor of the front parts, the face-to-face.

A faint tinkling of cries, of claws upon the wood floor: the cat, of which only the yellow eyes shine, slit with black; a dark blue wing that twitches against a black background where a blacker tail turns upraised.

The boy raises the girl to her feet, pushes her toward another ascending parquet passageway whose left wall opens onto a spiral staircase: the cat dashes toward it; the girl and the boy descend the staircase: the odor of the organ persists beneath the scent of the soapy hair. The dog shrinks back from the twisting steps, yelps, barks—the meat, where again?—retraces our path; will he trot through the rooms, hallway, stairhead, to the grand staircase?

Downstairs, it's a storage closet, high, narrow, with bicycles, scooters, pedal cars, stored away along a wooden wall, on a floor of dirt and unfinished concrete.

A door with a latch opens into the large room from which the going back in time began: at the center, amid the increased clamor from outside, the rope still trembles in the rose darkness, with a few flies on its fibers: there's a scratching at the door, where I can now see a rectangle of frosted glass in the middle, around the ornamented lock: Could it be my army mate, tapping with his tooth?

The girl, passing near the center of the room on the grand-staircase side, passes her hand over the rope, seizes the large stiff braid in her fist, brings it to her mouth, bites it; I see she has a pointed tooth in front between two beautiful well-shaped ones, and so I search for some other anomaly in the eyes that watch me, wide open, rose-white—the halo of a sunray comes through an opening in the indistinct background, from which the dog emerges, tail wagging with pleasure at having successfully descended the marble steps?

The boy—as I remain alone before her with her jaws on the rope—rasps a few low words against the frosted glass, receives, from outside, a few scraps of Picardy cusswords in reply, and partly opens the door-window: with hand on groin, my army mate, bare-chested, jacket and undershirt in fist, shifts on his feet at the threshold; a roar of motorcycles causes him to turn his head and torso; the girl sees the mark on his back, small overlaid lines of burns from the lighting that struck him as a child in a little copse in Amiénois—how is it possible that the lightning strike, together with his protruding tooth and his taste for coupling with animals (civilian criminal record in his military file), was not enough to exempt him from the draft and from service in Algeria?

Will he dare to enter into this space of the rich, of the "learned"?

Hunched slightly forward, between countenances of radiant joy, he puffs, growls, snorts, lets out a yelp, a call not of dogs but of humans, of those one hears in pens, stables, nanny goats and billy goats intermixed. Is he trying to tell us that he has just coupled with a nanny goat, or even a billy goat—but he would not have come out of it unwounded—or is he transforming himself into a semidomesticated animal to give himself the courage, or the right of the mentally, animally insane, to enter into this forbidden space?

The boy, his brow furrowed under black curls, sets the long fingers of his furry-wristed hand at his pocket against the knife; the girl now licks the frayed strands where she has gnawed at the fibers; my army mate enters, hairs on the front of his fatigues; his tooth presses against his red lip; the girl drops the rope, clutches the boy by the shoulders from behind; they step backward toward a large framed painting that rests against a clutter of wall hangings, vases, and small pieces of furniture: the colors are too dark to be able to make out a form, but the canvas is pierced at its center.

I feel a power seize my shoulders, strength gained for two years through live-fire exercises—machine gun, bazooka—bridge construction, worksites, lost again in prison, regained in the summer's work and in our autumn of dismantling, loading, unloading; my arms, my chest: this rope whose top can't be seen where a swallow and then another flit from beam to beam amid their tinkling cries, why, in the emptiness of this instant, the space of which I can already feel is bordered by a malignant power, of nature or of humans, why let this rope sway without seeing if I can climb it—I who in the obstacle-course drills passed by such ropes without touching them, making it known since my conscription that I refused to climb them, not because I lacked the strength, but because, since childhood, despite all that I read of various heroes in the jungle crossing rivers by the swing of a rope, I would only climb them for an armlength or two, without pleasure, as swimming and other activities sufficed.

But to show oneself to all, more visibly than on the ground, in the act of making an effort—when every act, of body, of mind, of heart, should be natural, immediately perfect, as the hand of the Creator, his word, sends forth finished creations—is impossible, except in cases of emergency, when the survival instinct should be sufficient.

Here, throwing his undershirt and jacket to the ground, my army mate throws himself at the rope, sniffs at its braid, its deposits from the afternoon; the girl mutters from the shadows; he drags his tooth along the strands; heartbeat doubled, I step forward, seize the rope pressed against his forehead; he moves aside; what would I gain by hoisting myself up a few meters on this dubious rope? I take hold of it with two hands, hoist myself up, cross my knees; the rope turns me, turns me again, sways me; my palms, calluses cracked by the barbed wire in August, scalded on the heavy equipment of the Corps of Engineers, burn once more on these tautened fibers; above, the little flights of the sparrows dislodge dust that falls on my forehead; the girl, down below, with the boy's hands on her bare shoulders, watches, a little bit of foam at the corners of her mouth: one breast is out; would climbing higher make her take the other one out too? I hoist myself farther upward, laughter comes to me, wild laughter shakes my chest; I must climb higher; I'm almost halfway up, the turning diminishes; stay longer at this height where the wild laughter, releasing all constraint, keeps me clasping the steadied rope with all my strength: So, without realizing it, I tricked my commanding officers, reputed to be good judges of youth, and tricked myself as well—could I also, then, in swimming, dive, and dive from higher...? Could I...could I...?

Climb higher, touch my skull to a beam, one of those where the swallows are panicking—more than two of them now?—my joints, my muscles, already sore at day's end, sustain the pulling and tugging even so...position my feet correctly, one above the rope, one below...I feel my dog tag against the bare skin of my chest and sliding across the hairs, cold amid the sweat: Should I pronounce its numbers again in my mind and, by this exercise of memory, distance myself from the effort of climbing, which I would wish to be as natural as that of a common monkey or, at least, of the Mowgli of long ago?

The dog, below, yelps, barks...who is clapping? She? Go back down: soles on the rope, skin at the edge of my palms already nearly torn; halfway down, I look: my army mate has come close to the girl, who smells an odor of ovine suint on him; the boy, backing away, crosses his hands in front of the girl's trembling chest as the creases of her crotch darken again; my crotch slides along the deposits from which the flies have detached themselves and disappeared; her mouth agape, I see the tip of her pointed tooth shine in the dusty ray of light; will he touch, with his long, slightly pruney fingers and painted nails, the goods of which he is the guardian: Her breast bared in its full expansiveness, the nipple, the mere thought of which makes me shut my eyelids to an inner and outer darkening?

With him too, the blood could come to his crotch, unless he has nothing there but the stub of an atrophied member.

Standing on the ground again: Will I feel strong enough now to go to the girl and touch her breasts? The wild laughter seizes me again; the cat, with the scraps of cartilage cracking between its teeth, comes back to purr between my ankles.

In the distance, a roar of motorcycles—along the Front de Mer? And toward what destination, in a country that has only one: Revolution?

A braying of donkeys, inland, the old world.

The girl, shaking herself free, draws her warm flesh, boned and boneless, near my own, now cooling, and wiggles it, takes my hands, opens one of them, lowers her mouth, sets her lips on my life line, ascends it with the tip of her tongue, her cheek brushes against the edge where the skin has been torn, the edges of her tongue linger there, her soapy curls touch my chin; should I grasp, clasp her at the back and pull her front toward my own ... the boy has slipped the knife out of his pocket again, opened the lock-blade; my army mate stamps his foot— is he doing it to call the nanny goat or billy goat to him and make it submit?—the boy passes his thumb over the edge of the blade, the girl pushes out her breasts; my army mate clasps his fists; did he, as a child, strangle the beast that resisted? That he threatens to do the same to the boy defers the motions of appeasement I have begun to make, eyes, mouth, hands; the girl, blade grazing her arm, leaps toward me, wraps her arms around me, eyelid, eyelashes batting against my cheek, finger already slipping through a belt loop of my fatigues, against my coccyx, those of her other hand searching where to set themselves down upon me (army jacket with objects in its pockets); the desire to protect her from the two of them, the one with his godless and lawless lust, the other with his passion for guarding her organ and her infirmity, and desire itself, my own, raw and vital, of which my member that rises in all its length is a mere simulacrum, accelerates the pounding of my too-large heart—*schweig still, mein Herz, schweig still*—of my arteries, my veins—wait until Paris, my neck, where she dips and raises her fresh mouth—to the back of my head.

I hear my army mate's breathing, with the ebb and flow of the froth on his lip around the tooth, his voice crystalline: "Go for it, Pierrot!" The roar of the motorcycles comes closer; machine-gun fire disperses it; the dog goes back to the tangle of scraps in the half-darkness, whimpers, farts; other dogs, outside, bark; he rushes toward the unlatched door, pushes it open with his paw, runs off into the little park; the cat sits perched in the half-light atop the tangled heap and licks its fur and claws; its eyes flash in the stirred-up dust. My army mate brings his palm to his well-stuffed nostrils, sniffs it: "This ain't nothin good for us, pal! Let's get outta here!" But we—the boy with the blade closed again and the knife put back in his pocket, the girl still pressed to me with all her breasts, my army mate with his jacket slipped on again, and me with the girl's feet on my feet—we advance toward the door; my mouth descends toward the girl's open mouth; at least, whatever happens, against my own, a pair of real lips—of which I believed, as a little child, that one kissing another was all it took to make a baby sprout in the belly of the bride.

A strong smell of gasoline presses back the scent of the bougainvilleas; black smoke rises into the pink sky; the singing of the little girls has ceased; sobs, cries come from the road; by a different route from the way we came, we walk hunched toward the road among cactuses: above the spines, the asphalt is in flames; farther on, motorcycles lying on their sides, wheels free, gasoline spilling from their pierced tanks; farther on, a single motorcycle, lying on its side, jolting, beneath the smoke, a belted body opened atop it, a leg quivering, the front wheel still spinning slowly; behind, in the middle of the pavement, a body, a young woman, very dark brown hair, blouse open, flower-print skirt bloodied, helmet trailing, advances on all fours along the asphalt where the fire burns out: the entire rim of her mouth is red—blood or lipstick smeared by the cries, the slobber, the tears? Without cover on the asphalt, in the remains of our uniforms, as the gunshots grow sparser inland: the girl shrinks against me as I hunch lower still, her nipples uncovered, translucent, among the spiny, bristly ears of the hacked and mutilated cactuses: bottles of antiseptic, bandages, are in the bathroom up there behind us, perhaps on the ground floor ... I straighten up ... but drop to the ground again ...

Klaxons: Algerian motorcycle cops, an ambulance, a 4x4 with armed men for protection; traffic stopped in both directions; the woman crawls forward on the soaked asphalt, nurses—a doctor in white?—kneel around the body of the young man whose head, blond—from an Alsatian family exiled to Algeria after the French defeat in 1870?—has already ceased to quiver, his face pallid beneath the doctor's pink gloves; the woman stands up on the asphalt, runs toward the group, pushes them aside, bends down, collapses onto the body, kisses the leg that quivers less and less, thrusts her mouth onto the man's large mouth; the pink glove repels her; a medic in a white smock jacket, black pants, grabs her shoulders, tugs at them; she keeps her mouth, her face, against the man's mouth and face where the doctor keeps his own and blows; my army mate, with his head between the boy's and mine, bleats softly; the leg, belted in leather, falls back to the asphalt; the woman, with her own swollen mouth, seals off the mouth where the death rattle slows; she holds between her palms the head that pitches sideways; the medic tugs at her hips; my shoulder, my armpit, the side of my chest grow wet with the tears of the girl as I clasp her head tight against me to muffle the sound of her sobs.

Wait for the body to be taken away, the young woman subdued, the motorcycles hauled to the ditch, then hoisted onto the coming vehicle? Make our way alongside the pavement until...? A bus, on its way down from Greater Kabylia, lets out its passengers, some turbaned, who scatter across the scene of the accident-attack, overwhelming the police officers; we, my army mate and I, decide, without words, eyes only, to step up onto the pavement where some very young soldiers of the Algerian Army—having emerged from an outlying marsh filled with trash, carcasses from El Harrach—finger their weapons... The rifle shots recede in the far distance among the first hills.

The girl, at my side, holds me back with her finger in a loop of my fatigues, in front this time, against the belt: this fresh hand near my member unstiffened by the sight of the agony that endures beneath the chest of the woman whose helmet has come to a halt before us as she thrusts her mouth toward the cast-back face, nearly blue in the pinkish gleam reflected in the spilled gasoline, and tries to receive, to swallow the last rattle of the agony; and the rage of our powerlessness, from the necessity of keeping under cover, push me to force open, to tear a sliver of Time so that I might pass through it, as childbirth pushed me out of my mother's womb, without mind or heart: Should I leave the girl, her mouth gaping at the mortal kiss upon the road—the woman covers the whole dying body with her own, hands to hands, legs to legs, the blood flows around the embrace; behind us, a hooting; the owl flies across the top of the little park again; the ambulance siren starts up, the revolving light too; a broader flow of blood beneath the belted black leather, near the loins—or close her mouth again with mine, which has opened itself, lips curling toward hers, the tips of our tongues touching in a pink porridge—where is this blood from? Her? Me? As if the body of the youth on the road had smashed itself, shattered, opened inside us.

Pull my lips away from hers, stand up straight, my army mate too, come out from among the cactuses, blend in as quick as we can among the closest group of turbanless civilians, farm laborers who have climbed down from the slatted sides of an open truck, vats swarming with flies on the truck bed? The boy—as I, standing straight and walking toward the road, look back—puts and holds both hands on the mouth of the girl who pushes froth and phlegm at his fingers; the dog, farther back, pushes his great bone along the grass.

My army mate and I thread our way through the groups to our passageway beneath the brambles, pass the barbed wire again; a few fellow soldiers, just out of the shower, cloth slung across their bare shoulders, climb to higher ground—the remains of a German fortification—to look at the accident-attack; we cross the courtyard, the drill grounds, the surroundings of the mess hall, the kitchens, toward the refectory where, in the din of voices, benches, and plates, those among us exempted from loading-duty are finishing their dinners; a lieutenant crosses the room, a folder of documents in his hand; we step behind a pillar.

Eat? Lose, from my lips, my teeth, the deposits of her saliva, her chewed meat, the froth of her rage, her contentment, her hope, her snot, her blood? Shower? Lose the salt of her tears, the marks from the touch of her hands, the rub of her cheeks against my own, against my shoulder, my neck, the sweat of her hand around mine as we stepped blind through those high rooms to the fluttering of the wings of the captive sparrow about to be devoured? From my chest, the imprint of her nipples?

The meat, black, sticks in my throat; the lieutenant crosses the room again, hand empty; one of us torments a chameleon whose foot he holds by a little string on the dirty oilcloth; the beast spits, activates its eyes, one upward, the other to the side... The folder, could it be open on the captain's desk, or even a colonel's? My arrest file? Interrogation file? My army mate's? His deviancies?

They let us talk and sing until late into the long night: Ph., his guitar; M., his nonviolence; P., his social architecture; my army mate, his Picard village dances, "Baby," Kondra...

When we go to bed, thirty of us in the barracks-room from regiments of the north and south and east and west, the moon, from the high little iron-grated windows, touches the lightning-flower on my army mate's curved back as he undresses, growls at the bedbugs in his meatsack: Will he flash his tooth at us when he turns around to let fly a fart? His shoulders, arms, hands, loins, chest, back, neck—it is from these that he must draw a livelihood, for himself, for others, and he holds them ready to act, grasp, carry, tug, lift, brandish, overturn, shove, embrace, push away.

On the other side of the pavement, from which gasoline, blood, and oil evaporate, in the grand villa about to be looted, where has the deprived boy put the girl to bed, and, having at least averted the danger to her crotch, where has he retired to, to doze off with one eye closed, the other keeping watch over the girl's organ, haunch, breast?

The barracks-room door, will it open to the MP lieutenant stepping through, alone or flanked by guards? Mice scurry beneath us from cot to cot, from scraps to scraps brought back from the refectory; my army mate, lying on his back, lets one mouse climb onto his palm, lets it run over his large mouth, slide its tail across his tooth, nibble at the La Vache Qui Rit that he eats each night before he falls asleep; but he sits up, claps his fist to his forehead, swings his feet over the side of the cot, rummages through the locker above him, takes out a little packet tied with string, pulls a photo out of the pocket of his army jacket, comes over to my bed, crouches down, unties the packet, takes out a few handwritten letters, a small blank pad of paper, a pencil: "The last scribble, you're goin' to write it fer me!" I slip out of my meatsack, sit on the edge of the cot, take the pad of paper, set it on my knees; he remains crouched, finishes chewing his portion of cheese; the mouse, "Germaine," scurries off to another bed, other food. My army mate places the photo before my eyes; me: "No need, pal, I'll write you your letter with my memory"; but still I look, for perhaps the thirtieth time, at the photo, scratched, sticky, of a girl's face, all teeth, slightly protruding, strong, with prominent nostrils, a flower—rose or carnation—tucked behind her ear beneath a wisp of dirty-blond hair. "You ain't even stiff fer her? Like fer the little mute...?" If I want to write him a heartfelt letter, the very last one, no less, I need a little desire... "It's me that dictates, it's me that's stiff!" he says, sitting at my side, his voice low but chiming; the two bunkmates are still playing cards at the back of the barracks; the chameleon makes its way among the smoke, darts its long tongue at invisible insects.

"My little mouse, what's she doin' at this hour?... Her sheets pulled up against her lips... she knows how to suck... wetting mine..."

"You'll see her for good in thirty days... live with her—the *petit bal*, that's finished. You want me to put what you're telling me?"

"No!... Put me some heart stuff, if it's ass stuff it'll get her hot fer others, not me..."

"I'm putting that she's your sun... by whose light we live... that you love no one but her, that she has to keep herself pure for you..."

"Except my mother, they wrote me I can go and see her now..."

"I'm putting normal things here..."

"Things they say in movies, in books?"

"Books, you mean photonovels?"

"Affirmative, like the *croques* say!"

"But you wipe yourself with those!"

"Put we'll make us some littl'uns climbin' all over the place..."

"Babies, you mean?"

"Lots of 'em, climbin' up on me... girls..."

"Girls, you want me to put that?

"Watch yourself, if I read any ass stuff you're no pal of mine anymore!"

I write; at each line, he nudges me with his hip; the little noise of the froth at his protruding tooth marks his breaths; the letter finished, but signed by him, he reads over the words he can read, wets the envelope, folds, slips the photo in, returns to his cot, shuts the letter inside his locker, and collapses, asleep, snoring already, on the straw mattress; on the table oilcloth, the chameleon wavers among the smoke of the troop; Baby Soap prepares his body for sleep, smiles, in front of his mirror, at the girls from the village dances.

The youth, on the road, is he truly dead? Do we see with full mind—here, from our extraterritorial military ground—the things that happen on the civilian side of the pavement? The quivering leg, the pallor that seizes the whole face, lips, eyes, of one already summoned to appear before the divine tribunal... the mouth flowing with tears that seals the mouth from which the young woman, biting, keeps the emergency doctor's mouth away.

Keep all of her on me! The trace of her glance upon my skin, upon my eyes: fall asleep without touching it.

How, free in the home country, or even tomorrow already, here or in the port where a few tons of material still remain to be loaded into the cargo holds, could I find out more about the villa, about her? Is she sleeping now, or is the boy at pains to quiet her on her bed? The fold of the shorts against the organ, the haunches that roll over on the sheet, the buttocks that round themselves out to her frothy muttering into the pillow... the breasts, so fragile, spill onto the folds of the sheet... Do people speak, do people hear in her dreams? I bend my head toward hers; she buries her face in the pillow; her haunches shudder, she unburies her awakening face, mute laughter shakes her, breasts thrust out; in the ray of moonlight, her open hands grope for my lips, my eyes...

In the morning, as I pass our captain in a corridor, I look him in the eyes, just long enough and with enough intensity to make sure he doesn't have anything against me beyond the usual grievances under which I still live.

Our rank falls in with others, wobbly-legged—rifles, cartridge belts, canteens, tin cups on their packs—on the ballast in front of the opening of the steamer's cargo hold; groups of civilians, families, lean out, high up, over the ship's rails; the children with their chins on the ropes, the women with handkerchiefs at their eyes; above the quay, youths perched or seated or crouched on the parapets cock their arms at us; police officers order them down. At the far end of the quay a form advances along the cobblestones, a legless turbaned man moving on his trunk and fists, erect member protruding from the bottom of the leather cassock rigged together around the nub of his thighs. Wind and clouds advance from the Great South—which we can sense is out of France's hands, nature too powerful to be subjugated.

The steamer turns in the setting sun; we settle ourselves, a few hundred of us, on the planks of the hold; the large cookpots, held by two men in aprons, are already making the rounds from one company to the other, steaming: beans and boiled meat; eat so as to vomit less—a storm has been announced for the middle part of the crossing.

Off the coast of Minorca, many vomit—but to suffer on the way back to liberty is cause for laughter amid the vomit and the flows of gruel spilling under the kitchen doors; the officers are quartered above, but they are sailing toward opprobrium.

Discipline having grown slack, I make my way toward the deck, breathe in the violent sea air with its rapid clouds and covered stars. Dry storm, whirlwinds heavy with Saharan sand. I step out onto the deck, I hear the crash of the waves against the stern; above, the fitful plumes rise from one or two smokestacks; down below and along the hull, the engine growls; pitch and toss, but I do not vomit; other soldiers, having come up from below, shirts torn at their chests by the gusts, fling words; I hold my glasses against my nose at the base of my brow.

Among ropes, straps, pipes, cabinets, a sleeper lies on a chaise longue, then two sleepers, then families, covered in shawls and blankets, suitcases at their feet, under the canvas of the deck chairs, on the chaise-longue footrests; a suitcase opened on the decking spills forth hard objects, fine linen; a hand at the end of a pale arm gathers them up, puts them back, presses shut the clasps; a shod foot pushes the suitcase into a corner; a dark hand clasps the pale hand; two heads bend toward each other in the shifting darkness; I can hear a kiss—quiet—which a swerve of the steamer bursts.

Small children, two boys and a girl, having climbed down from the heap of thighs and small suitcases and blankets, tumble about on the decking, steady themselves on their hands and knees, crawl toward opened biscuit tins, the scattered contents already picked through by the muzzles of dogs trailing leashes.

Sitting on a hatch, soldiers—from our military region—ties undone, gentian at their epaulettes, fourragères at their shoulders—selected, France's pride, to lead the ranks when we disembark in Marseille?—drink beers and *"couilles"* of Orangina; one of them, black-skinned, takes a little flute out of his unbuttoned jacket and plays a motif from the south that he extends into a delicate, pleading melody. Above, the clouds slow down, pile together, black; a revolving beam from the pilothouse lights up the deck, alternates upon his curled lip, his throat that swells, unswells; his head tilts back, little flute pointing at the black mass beyond which the hurricane growls, bursts: by day, in summer, on solid ground, above the wheat fields, it would be "the devil is bowling"; by night, at sea, caught between two masses, above, below, what God, what god—not even Neptune, the Mediterranean's familiar—could withstand this? Is the little flute trying to summon another hurricane, down below, in Africa, forest, desert, savanna? Little sprite of furrow, jar, or infant's bed, quieting the tempest with a ruse?

The downpour begins; everyone scatters, slips beneath the tarps; is my lightning-struck army mate trembling in the hold amid his vomit?

Under the large black tarp where I take shelter, lightning hitting at the folds, I turn on my pocket lamp: children asleep on an overcoat, thumbs in their mouths, an old man, in a jacket, still seated, his arms on his knees, a young woman, her head in the nook of her elbow, her hair in a kerchief, lying on her side, haunch in a light flower-print dress that her hand tucks beneath her; the black soldier slips under, takes up his little flute again, plays it very quietly; the old man, Légion d'Honneur ribbon on the lapel of his threadbare jacket, pencils in his breast pocket, grabs me by the arm: "...You didn't defend us, did you? You didn't defend us...they lied to you, you too"; a heave sends us all spilling on top of each other; the little flute rolls along the soaked decking; the black hand pursues it; a calm: the old man stretches himself out, falls asleep; I stretch myself out next to the soldier in dress uniform who, head on the floor, plays again; a heave flings us toward the stern, my head against the heels of the young woman who, from a dream, hitches up her dress; the legs open; my heart pounds again as at the breasts of the girl; from within a tangle of thin pink fabric, a swelling; the faint light disappears; only a fringe of fleece can be seen, blacker than the darkness; a shudder from the young woman tips the swelling to the side; a red fingernail slips into the slit, spreads it, from the pink flesh veined with red a secretion glistens; a shudder again, the young woman hitches the fabric of her sodden dress higher; the organ appears, touched by the pink fabric, entire, the two parts and the fleece; higher, crinkled, slightly moist, in the creases of the thighs is the little fold of pink linen narrowed against the left thigh: What fingers in the full darkness are tugging at it? A breathing, beside her, a man's muttering, a smell of smoke; I peer into the hollow of the thigh, a man's finger, yellowed, moves forward there, advances toward the mound, thrusts its short nail into it, thrusts itself a third of the way inside, folds back what reveals itself as a lip opening to another lip, beneath; a deeper roll of the ship makes the nausea rise into my teeth: Should I come out from under the tarp to vomit over the ship's rail? If I move, my head comes out from between the young woman's heels, the man sees me...my conscience condemns me for gazing upon, knowing, a secret, but for fear that the man might find cause for a brawl that would jeopardize my liberation, I fix my eyes on the forbidden place, where the movement of the finger should focus my attention on something stronger than the need to vomit; but since childhood I live each vision so intensely that, by immediately rooting it in a historical, metaphysical, origin, and by extending it almost simultaneously into a future resolution or metamorphosis, I cause its present center to explode, and so the vision disappears within me, to transform itself there into objects of creation, and erases itself from exterior reality.

The little flute plays, its volume changing with the movement of the waves, then slips from the hand, rolls on the decking; the soldier, head cast back, has fallen asleep; the old man moves his jaws.

A calm; I come out on my knees from under the tarp; vomiting impossible, spasms; the lights of Minorca, under the rule of a dictator at the time, the first lights of Europe, appear in the hushed darkness; Orion, Cassiopeia shine in the clear sky, a royal mantle in which my ear hears a rustling as of a hand: "My beloved Son, in whom I am well pleased"; large birds cross the great halo of the naked moon, cry out. Other soldiers, against orders—no contact with the repatriated—have gone up on deck and are smoking cigarettes, lips and nostrils soiled with vomit.

From under the tarp heavy with rain, the man emerges, supple-backed, tall, the pink jersey of a Belcourt football club stretched tight against his big-nippled chest, his hand on the necks of the wobbling children; I see his yellowed finger shine; the young woman, even more supple, breasts partly bared, lifts the fabric of the tarp over the stooped old man who, reddened eyes, white hairs on his neck, straightens up, breathes, and rejects the hand of the woman whose gaze meets mine, and I turn away: Would my eyes show her that I've seen her organ from up close—so near I had to hold my breath not to smell the slit, the fleece—and the husband's finger letting itself be caught in it: her large eyes pale blue; her laundry scent, her curly hair spilling out of her flower-print kerchief, her haunch moving, easy, between her hips, from one traveler's bag to the next, rejecting with a little flick of her arched loins the venturesome hands; the children sway from side to side, peer up at the stars and at the fourragères of the uniforms; one of the children lets his gaze linger in mine, from which I've removed my glasses; I have seen the organ that birthed him, which his father will penetrate again with his member as if to pull other children out from that animal tangle of open flesh, of hairs caressing the fetus as it comes out, and closing up again, behind, as the waters of the Red Sea closed upon evil.

The soldier, having come out from under the tarp, takes up his little flute again—soon, at liberty, in my room or in nature, play again the flageolet I received for my ninth birthday, in which I soothed the breath of my rage—and plays under the brightening sky, where the earthy scents of Africa give way to those of the sea alone.

In sight of France's mainland shores, we have to go down into the hold, rejoin our sections and companies, squelch through the puddles of vomit as the steamship turns and comes to a stop with thuddings, listen again, cheeks spattered with bits of vomit, to the orders of sub-officers and officers coming fresh-cheeked from their cabins, take up our rifles from the racks again, helmets, line up, wait—all requests for information met with suspicious rage—step forward, duffel bags dragged along the planks, behind the infantry marines, past the bolts drawn back at the doors, toward the gangways laid above the eddying water; one of us, during the wait, has taken his chameleon—a gift from a fellow soldier stationed in the south—out of a side pocket of his large pack from which seeps a flow of wild honey, and having set the chameleon, leg tied, upon his shoulder, in the haste of disembarking he drops the string; the chameleon clutches at the epaulette but falls into the sea, flails there around the string, sinks into the deep; the little gray-green saurian—born in some guelta in Tassili n'Ajjer whose pristine waters slaked the thirst of Garamantes chariot drivers thousands of years ago—now plummets where impure predators lie in wait, in these local waters filled with oil waste, carcasses, detritus of marital brawls.

Lined up on the quay again, orders issued without explanations, we march past, then step in formation to Camp Sainte-Marthe.

Earth, sky, lusterless, scentless. We are pushed toward the dormitories; the hammocks still sway on their chains, dirtied by regiments already transported by train toward the eastern camps: once we have settled ourselves, we are sent to the refectories: stools, cookpots, glass dinner plates, bromide-laced wine, meanderings outdoors in the nightfall among the huts; from the cooks, we learn that starting tomorrow we'll be in the port to unload our equipment and load it onto the trains; to bed, in the stacked hammocks, last vomitings, dreams—collective by now, through the lack of privacy, repeated words, thoughts prohibited?

Early in the morning, hop into the trucks, sleep a little longer sitting against the side slats; at the port, hop from the trucks; our ship's cargo hold is open: we have to take back out of it the pieces that we transported into it and fastened in place in Algiers; load them onto the trucks; at the trains, begin to lift and slide and lug them into the freight cars; six days of work, barehanded, amid the rust, the oil, the clatter. At the end of it, we are granted an evening of temporary leave: a few of us, in light dress uniform with epaulettes, gentians, fourragères at our shoulders, "tarte" berets on our heads, go down by bus to the Vallon des Auffes, to a workers' restaurant.

In the city, groups of families carrying bags and suitcases outside short-term rental apartment buildings. In the middle of one of the groups, a girl wearing a dress growls, huffs, snorts, from beneath a pink straw hat; my heart pounds in its only limb—but already because she would be a reapparition, a repetition, therefore fatal (in the image of Eurydice annulled by Orpheus's gaze as he looks back at her), a fatal uprooting from that interior abyss where, since childhood, I have given life to every living thing that I have seen outside myself—beings, acts, places, Gods—with a purpose that became clearer to me with and through my taste for words when I began to translate the ancient texts—but now, so far from Paris, from all literature, and caught since my incarceration in such a single-minded drive toward my deliverance from servitude, do I still think of the desired oeuvre?

At the bus stop, she looks back: if her eyes stay upon me, it is her—although, taking after my mother, I've always attracted the eyes and the affection of the impaired and, later, of the oppressed.

Standing in the bus that fills with people, hand on the strap, I hold her eyes in mine, then lower them onto her partly bared shoulders beneath the halter of the dress; over the curve of her cheek and, as she turns away, over her nape; the more I gaze at her, copy of her or she herself, the more my being comes undone, implodes, and the more I stagger, the ground we all possess slips away to others; what I can see of the sky isn't mine anymore; life, as repetition, isn't worth it; only the first time counts. And its commensurability with the universal reality of the instant, the movement of our star among the others, the infinite microscopicness of all matter.

Recompose myself as a young soldier of the nation of France and the continent of Europe, close to his liberation, in the company of others, flesh and bone and blood—and seed. As the child of a God in whom I still slightly believe, metamorphosis creating them all. Constrained, temporarily, to a limited reality, like the flies with their large eyes, like dogs with their aching penises—and who are we to affirm, century after century, that our life is worth more than theirs: seen from very high above (but how high is very high?) we swarm about like the ants that frighten us or the insects that we set on fire.

As for seed, it's as if I no longer have any: not having been able, for more than two years, to bring it out of myself as text.

But, from among the grouped family, her plump little hand in front of her eyes raises and lowers three of her fingers, of which I now see that one is missing; her light dress, almost mauve, clings to the small of her back and pelvis; higher up, the breasts, more swollen than on the one from the African coast; all washed here, among others whom she does not bite, her teeth not having torn the straw of her hat, her eyes, in which I search for the wound in the right iris, fix themselves in mine, barely visible behind my lenses, fogged by the breaths of the passengers cramped, suffocated by the flood of the repatriated. Could it be that the one from over there, the abandoned land—the one whom I can scarcely speak of as "she," for her nature so contradicts the word—by means of a double, is trying to draw my attention to her fate, which the worry for my own has overshadowed? And should I respond, with even a blink of my lashes, to soothe her, perhaps at this moment strapped down and writhing on a restraint bed? A rush of the crowd spurs the bus to start off again toward the seafront.

From the arch of the Monument aux Armées d'Orient, we descend into the little port enclosed by a high triple-arched bridge: *pointus* and pleasure boats return to the quays among the odors of rotting fish, gasoline, and frying oil; no more Arabs or Berbers among the reanimated clamor in the darkness of the premature sunset behind thunderclouds.

Bouillabaisse for the whole table: facing me is my toothy army mate, who trembles at the approaching storm; his protruding tooth presses his lip so hard it bleeds. My bowels troubled by the change from military to civilian food, I go up to look for the toilet on the wooden upper story against the rocks; downstairs, as they await the main course, Ph.'s guitar plays an Andalusian Istikhbar motif, a dreamy prelude at the end of which, instead of strumming the rhythm of a dance, he begins the prelude again: no theme; only arpeggios; for us, waiting for liberation, for the reentering into life, the true life, outside of domination.

On the slats of the passageway, a girl, small, still in her skimpy two-piece bathing suit, tight below, loose around the large, nicely raised breasts, leans against the railing, white towel over her shoulders and around her neck, she shakes off the salt that shines on her full forms, hardly tanned, in the red setting sun between the dark cloud masses now bearing down on the Frioul archipelago; she pushes out her tongue, licks along the rise of her lips; her haunches quiver against the bars from a movement that comes from her nape, half-hidden beneath the towel. My tongue, too, pushes out between my lips, beneath my still aching nostril from which blood still seeps from when I get up to when I lie down. A gust of wind heavy with warm rain sways the walkway; amid the shuddering, below the bit of fleece that flares between her thighs toward her navel, the fabric folds upon the organ, molds it into two parts beneath the downpour that soaks it.

I enter into the stall, crouch on the planks above the hole: below are rocks among which frothy eddies stirred up by the wind of the gathering thunderstorm churn bottles, tin cans, trash of copulation. Ever since I discovered as a child that others defecate, any person—respectable, illustrious, adult—that I have seen, met, gazed upon in real life or in newspapers, biographies, has immediately been "extended" into their defecation, not thereby reduced in grandeur, but reinforced in their noble human misery among others of their kind, straining to excrete; any person seen eating, extended into their upcoming defecation; and in the very rare luxury restaurants to which I have had the occasion to be brought, the more the swallowed dishes are of superior quality, "prized," of beautiful appearance and hue, the more immediate is their extension into excrement, punishment for the offense of having spent on them the sum of so many months, years, of hard labor for others. I have to restrain myself from subjecting Christ, the Virgin Mary, certain other saints and mystics to the travail of defecation. Historical figures, ancient, medieval, modern, contemporary, emperors, kings, princes, great commanders, great ministers, heroes, heroines, politicians seen or heard from near or far—all have "bowel movements," and they lose no parcel of their prestige in doing so. Christ defecating among the rocks of Galilee, this or that king perched upon his commode, this or that great man pulling the cord upon his excretions—familiar images, inquiries. With the women, from Antigone, or even Eve or Judith, to Joan of Arc, George Sand, or Marie Curie, I falter and quickly turn away my thoughts; is it possible that the Virgin Mary, having conceived without fleshly act, was also exempted from ... dress gathered up, defecating at a distance from Joseph's wood shavings—but to every ingestion, a defecation; food cannot keep itself entirely within the body, without risk of explosion.

My entire crotch thrills at that fold of fabric wet against the quivering of the organ stretched from the right part to the left: but a golden fly that has zizzed around me in the half-darkness since I entered here now alights on the circumcised glans of my stiff member, tucked against my belly: the tickling makes me laugh wildly. I hear a sliding of flesh against the door: Is it her thigh, in whose hollow the hem of the bikini bottom rises into the fleece? Has she taken shelter beneath the awning of the suspended stall, where the downpour spatters amid the noise of the still distant thunder? Are my army mates keeping an eye on my beret, rolled up beside my plate?

Finished and wanting to come out, I gently push at the door against which the flesh is pressed: foreseeing that I'll have to have doings with this flesh, heart pounding in my ears and lurching, I take off my glasses, tuck them into the breast pocket of my jacket, to appear with my face as nature made it, without these glasses—from my childhood reading by dormitory night-light—that are my separation from living people; I push; I sense a displacement of perfume, suntan lotion, sweat, rain, salt; I cannot see past the tip of my nostrils; I advance beyond what must be the opened door, advance toward the heart of the fragrance in this fog which is the falling night, reach out my hand; it touches the railing to the right, which it grasps, but the halo of flesh shifts toward it from the left, with a little throaty laugh above; the door fully opened against the railing, I reach forth my other hand, grope about: the less I can see, the more my member stiffens; a hand, dainty, fresh, large, forthright, clasps my wrist, draws it toward the center of the silhouette, which my eyes can hardly discern: the little laugh comes from between lips that, from two heads away, I cannot see; I smell an odor of pâté, of fresh bread, lipstick; the hand spreads my fingers and presses them against the swell of flesh that throbs quickly beneath the very thin fabric; my little finger, attempting to free itself, touches a tuft; the bikini bottom, rolled down—before I came out from the stall, or now?—lays bare the thick fleece; close to me, her mouth cast upward toward mine, it's as if her breathing were now coming from her breasts, through her nipples which she presses against my chest.

Two of my fingers, beneath three of hers, remain on the swell, molded, firm; the thunder cuts across the bridge; flashes of lighting let me see her forehead, domed, her painted eyelashes, her green eyes with their intense whites, her irises where shifting reflections pass as our fingers sink or rise in the mound; her other hand descends beneath my belt; will she unbuckle it like the middle-aged woman with violet lips at the "Sphynx" in Algiers, against the wall, in the come-and-go of the elevators loaded with scum bedecked in shoulder stripes? Will she unbutton me? Her fingers rise, rise again over the large fold my member makes there.

The fingers of my other hand set themselves upon her haunches, her back, between her shoulder blades, against her nape where, weaving themselves amid the wet hair, they open wide to scratch the scalp—the swell of flesh grows softer beneath my fingers under hers—then caress it, envelop it, the sweetness of a part of myself, exhausted by the self-to-self in the constant lack of privacy, caressed by this unfamiliar hair, fresh, thick, tender, on a head just out of adolescence, and the hopes that crowd there, take shape there...

Take out my glasses again to see, not only close up, but also around, behind, before, far into the dark height, downward where ebb and flow grow stronger: eye to eye, almost mouth to mouth, I draw my fingers out from the hair, slip them into my breast pocket; the frame has caught on an inner seam; I tug; her fingers descend, wrist still rubbing the girth of the member between my thighs; I rummage through my pocket; with an odor of fish, her breath flows against my earlobe, her voice at last, crystalline, accented, quivering with her little laugh: "Pull it out for me!" Does she want a cigarette from the pack she thinks I'm trying to pull out of my pocket? The top of her cheek twitches below the eye socket; on this swaying walkway in this darkness that my scant vision can tell is not only that of the thunderstorm but also that of the fallen night, the meaning of her words hits my heart, I advance, I rush my mouth to hers, the jaws of which open: open my mouth at last, open my heart at its root, unfurl my lips, without fear of ridiculousness, for an act of pure present, future annulled.

Lightning more and more dazzling; rolling thunder; a clamor below; cries of everyone running for shelter, chairs upturned, crashing plates.

Our jaws, unequal, knock against each other; our tongues seek each other, each with its wounds, its bumps, its raspy power, they rise up against each other, coil between our cheeks; saliva of a woman, saliva of a man, pâté to pâté: her tongue swells against mine; her fingers, slipping between my buttons, rummage through my tufted hairs grown thick already, as on my chest and everywhere; the fake mother-of-pearl bracelet that hangs from the base of her wrist gets snagged on the rise of the scar on my glans and its member, which she tugs with all her fingers, which resists...

Thunder above; my hand still rummages in my pocket, lightning illuminating the entire port that I see as if my vision had been restored: glare of the lightning, cosmic, substituting for my poor visual capacity as a deficient human; saliva drools from our single mouth, a sucker alive with its own breath; by the taste of her saliva I retrace her day back to the moment she woke up, her mouth encircled with crusts of restless sleep, of chewing on dream delicacies, of cinema trysts...

Crash, smoke, odor of fire; the lightning has struck an adjoining wooden balcony, a palm tree that I see in the gash of light bend, unbend its blackened fronds; in our mouths, before the taste of ashes, the savor of lighting. A poisoning in our saliva? A taste of atoms, the splitting of atoms... The savor of God's wrath, of what our humankind, our planet, our star will become when, colliding with another or consumed, it explodes?

From down below, the odor of fire dissipating, a great hiccup, shrill wheezings, a crash, a sound from the guitar, our mouths unjoin, her bared breasts, whose nipples now free themselves from the folds of my jacket, move to the swaying of the footbridge in the lessening downpour: Leave without touching this beautiful fruit, without biting into it? Add this pleasure to the hope for an imminent but precarious deliverance? Find a place to go further? Stay standing here, or make the most of the trembling slats to drop to the ground and embrace, penetrate, knead the girl who ... arms raised, tufts beneath her armpits, rubs her scalp again with the towel?

But her panting chest, her hurried glances toward the rock face where the sprawling eatery comes to an end near the top—a hallway? A landing? A storage closet where she might pull out the remains of a sofa, a mattress, on which to fall back, she, underneath me, spreading herself entirely?

Another rub of her hair and, with the wheezings downstairs changed into cries in which I recognize the voice of my toothy army mate, and the girl having detected an odor of shit on my hand, I detach myself from her, take my glasses out at last—one lens unrepaired since the interrogation—put them back on, retrace my steps along the slats toward the stairs, go down to the bottom: on the terrace, under the awning flapping and tearing itself in the wind, my army mate, on all fours, his tooth scraping the concrete as others thump at his back, expels a fishbone as long as his fourragère; he lifts his red face to me, tears, slobber, already bloody vomit; down below, on the rocks, the guitar still resounds, dismantled.

Crouching, I gently pull at the fishbone as he strains, wheezes, moans ("Pull it out for me..."); in the dining room where the waiter has pushed him, hunched over on his knees, a washbasin beneath his chin, the fishbone emerges completely; from the far end of the blackout-darkened room, the girl appears, her hand slipping her top over her breasts, uncovering as she covers them, her bikini bottom rolled a little upon the fleece, her eyes glinting in the last flashes of the lightning; another passageway, another flight of stairs to the walkway; she fills a tall glass with hot water at the bar and, to the faint rustling of her bathing suit which I can hear among the rumblings of the last thunder, she steps forward, barefoot, ribbons around her ankles, crouches down in front of my army mate stretched out now on a sofa; his protruding tooth below my wrist, I cradle his scalp with one hand, with the other I show him again the fishbone that a child in rompers, having come running to fetch his toys, tries to grab; from the shallow breaths the girl takes between my palm and the toothy one's mouth, and by her smile, brief then broad, I realize she can smell on my palm or fingers a trace of my defecation and wiping upstairs; and that, even more than our mingled mouths and her little hand on my member, this odor binds us to each other: What more secret thing could I conceal from her, or she from me, than to smile and keep smelling this odor with tilted head? What more could she hide from me? Since an embrace is a mixing of secrets, do we now make love? Me holding the fishbone, frothy, long, between my fingers, her breath changes to voice, to words, fresh, from between her lips, stretched back toward her dimples: "You pulled it out for me!" My army mate drinks; her top, untied at the back, slides over, under, her breasts; blood reddens the water in the glass, the toothy one's teeth clinking against the rim; a soaked mop strikes the haunch of the girl who, handing me the glass, straightens up as a furry hand refastens her top between her shoulder blades; an odor of life rises from her bikini bottom, shaken with rage; the curly auburn hairs of her fleece spring to life, bristle up; the mop slides along her haunch; through my lenses, the cracked one doubling my vision, I can see a large male body, potbellied, a chest molded by a worn cotton undershirt, a scar that the electricity of the thunderstorm has made more red beneath the bared navel; we have to rise to our feet; the man, rag over his shoulder, mop tossed into the bucket, turns up an uneven mustache with his finger; the fingers of his other hand grip the nape of the girl who, with her eyes in mine, arches her loins against him; the cloth of her bikini bottom creases: Would I be worth as much?

To live for a few minutes in the Other... As a young child, after the war, large head, skinny legs with round-boned kneecaps jutting out, before I learned numbers, the very long ones, at the end of primary school and, at the same time, from my family—echoing the numbers of the Old Testament that we learned in our mother's voice—the numbers of the murdered, the massacred, the annihilated, I would daydream of being able to know all humans, one by one or family by family, of entering into their lives for at least the span of a small child's afternoon. Numbers, first through the image of the animals of the ground and of the air, then by the account of the "displaced persons" in Europe and Asia for whom we prayed each evening—millions of surviving beings, families, children searching for each other over the face of the Earth, multitudes imagined as far as a child's eye can see—reinforced by the study of arithmetic and the digits I could begin to read at the back of my primers, transformed this vague dream into an enchanted tale, by the end of which, as it was still impossible for me to imagine myself alive beyond the time of my child body, I had to give up the idea of visiting all the households in the world, of meeting along the roads children and old men and women leading me into their houses, lost little girls reunited with their mothers, adult orphans finding their mothers and fathers, holy men bringing me to their hermitages, holy women to their dispensaries, wanderers to their hovels, fowlers to their birds, fishermen to their boats, victims to their torturers…

Our last night in the rusty-chained hammocks that clank to our nightmares or dream embraces.

Departure in the blue half-darkness of dawn; at the Gare de La Joliette, we climb into the passenger cars of the trains onto which we have loaded our heavy equipment; three days and three nights of rocking back and forth—with no information except our goal: Sissonne-en-Champagne—along the Rhône Valley, where thousands of ill-loved repatriated persons still crowd the stations, waiting for the municipal and departmental social services to take them in charge. Through our dirty, scratched windows, between slumber, bread-breaks, rations, beers, card games, lengthy jokes becoming more and more dreamlike as we approach the region of this or that soldier's actual or supposed fiancée, we gaze at the autumn landscapes, dry and white up to Orange, more and more green and tawny toward Lyon and then Dijon. At least, if I am kept beyond my term, will I be closer to those who could protect me?

In the Gare d'A., where we remain at a halt for one night to allow the repatriated-persons trains to pass, I step off the train with my snag-toothed army mate, his throat cauterized but sore, to buy something to drink for our drowsy group: in the press of the crowd, my arms loaded with beer and "couilles" of Orangina, I see a young woman in a white blouse beneath a tailored jacket, the brim of her hat casting a shadow over her eyelids and the top of her cheeks, her lips open to call out, her high forehead furrowed: Could it be the one whose organ I smelled beneath the tarp aboard the steamer, and whose face I only glimpsed as we began to disembark at La Joliette? Now she lifts her hand above her eyes under the harsh neon lights of the hall. Is she looking for her husband whose index finger I came to know at sea? A child?

Taking a mirror out of the purse at her wrist, she looks at herself, calls out, looks at herself, takes out a little powder case and pad, calls out, powders her cheeks, nostrils, forehead; in the shifting clamor, I can make out a little of her voice, clear, accented—yes, she's from over-there—imperious, then plaintive... then, from among the shift of odors, cinders, hot iron, a scent arrives, already ancient for me, from another life, before, the scent of the powder we continued to carry to my bedridden mother so that, with feebler and feebler hand, she could pat her more and more translucent face before any visitor entered... My arms tremble and the glass clinks; on her wrist is a little bandage, slightly reddened, along the vein; a wound incurred during the repatriation journey; the movement of the powdering and of the lips opening to call out accelerates; the little wound—could she be a survivor of the Oran Massacre of July 5, wounded there defending herself when, led out of the station among those carried off in vans and delivered to the rioters, she lifted her arm before a brandished axe? But, finding no boat in Oran, had she managed to flee to Algiers, by road or by Inox, book a ticket there, alone or with her children, her husband having found her again, but sanity lost. How, during the station stop, could she have gotten off the railway car, escaping the nurses and orderlies in the press of the crowd? As I make my way toward the platform, I collide with a thickset man, necktie, light-colored suitcase with gold fittings slung from his shoulder; he goes to the young woman, puts down the suitcase, sets his foot on it, slips his arm around the woman's waist, takes the powder case out of her hand and puts it back into the little purse at her wrist; takes her other wrist, kisses it on the bandage; a great quivering of the shoulders, and she buries her tearful face, but her free hand reopens the clasp of the purse, takes the powder box out again; the mouth against the chest opens, calls out...

The downpour strikes the roofs of the pre-World War II railway cars as we pass into Champagne in the falling night: the convoy slows its pace in a narrow valley where a high footpath borders a thick field of rotting corn; on this path run several young girls, hands on their hats; the top of the window comes up to above their hats; I watch their faces, their shoulders, their breasts bound bouncing pouring wet; the others, from down below, watch their legs, their thighs against which they hold their gathered-up flower-print dresses: From what festival, civil or religious, could they be returning? What day is it? Sunday? Or what feast day? All Saints'? Returning from the graveyard? Saturday? Returning from the village dance? The blackened grass conceals their shoes from us: since the window is kept closed, we can only hear little muted fragments of what their open mouths cry to us, between the clatter of the convoy on this seldom-used track and the patter of the rain; but I hear their nearly choked breathing—laughter, sprint—beating against their chests from within, the shaking of their breasts molded by the soaked fabric; they now take up the entire window; one of us unbuttons himself, presses his member against the glass; they veer to the right between two fields.

The more the night thickens, the more the convoy slows; at a still lit station, on a siding, near what appears in the darkness as a long and high dunghill whose reek wafts to us through the vestibules, the train hiccups and comes to a stop; this is where we have to roll out our duffel bags on the slats, many of which are rotting; from what kitchen have come these cookpots that we go out to fetch in the diminishing rain, on a railway platform, steaming? Who brought them, fellow soldiers from what regiment?

No ladle; should we dip into them our dented cups still covered in khaki cloth?

Where to defecate? No latrines in the troop cars; in broad daylight, at the stations in the Rhône Valley, the wait for the toilets, filled with children excited by the hasty journey, was so long that most of us found hiding places among the machines, the defunct railcars, holes in the railway bed; here, at the great manure heap in the rain, behind barbed wire, beyond a crossable trench, with swine wriggling, grunting, squealing in the pigsties, cows farting in the sheds, lights of farmhouses and villages switching off, we defecate, members raised, beneath the flights of the owls; the soup no sooner gulped than shat.

Our words, poor, repeated, our onomatopoeias, our scraps of army Arabic, our strainings, intertwine with the sounds of the beasts, the bellowing of the oxen, the bleating of the goats; uncrouched, we climb back into the cars, which will remain at a halt in the station until dawn; the officers assign guard duty for the night: under the cleared sky, cold hands on the rifle strap, we patrol the length of the heavy-equipment cars.

... As a child, stretched out in the grass of fields, embankments, or floating on the surface of ponds or of the ocean, I watched the skies, the seat of the past, the future, antiquity, anticipation, until my adolescence, when poetry replaced them with its own constellations; since my first nights of guard duty in watchtowers, worksites, outposts, resettlement camps, deprived of poetry, of art, I have begun to watch the skies again, though I will soon see almost nothing of them from city streets and through curls of smoke.

The railcars smell of grease, oil, rust, metal: What cars are the NCOs and the commissioned officers quartered in? We only have our corporals with us.

Last gruntings, squealings, mooings, toward the manure heap where some army mates linger, try to start duos and trios with the beasts.

On the other side of the tracks, toward the open countryside where I can make out a surface of water in the halo of moonlight, the sound of a wood-and-metal gate being opened: a perfume advances toward the tracks—a woman, women, in the darkness? Or attackers, misting perfume to trick the guards? What terrorist group would have any use for this heavy equipment? Or could it be to take revenge on soldiers who fanatics claim supported, on orders of the head of state, the rebel takeover?

A blond hairdo appears between two bushes, a pale upper bosom; I finger my trigger.

The hairdo retreats; another appears to the left of the bushes, a heel taps against the track; three women in black and red, breasts forward, cross the rails; my throat pulses beneath the chain of my dog tag: I hold my weapon lowered; one of the three twists, turns her hips, the back of her ring-bedecked hand at her tight-clad waist, is this a dream? A scene from a film without the theater? On the other side of the train, the gruntings diminish, laughter rises from my groin; I know, from the letters I wrote for some of them, the poverty of these soldiers—like my own (basic pay, barter)—ten of them put together couldn't come up with the cost of a prostitute for one; only lightly clad beneath lined raincoats, have the women come on foot from some nearby city? Did a car deposit them on a back path, the pimp, white loafers at the pedals, smoking a cigarette in the shadows...?

Me, weapon loaded, holding unarmed women "at bay." But, on their side, worse than a weapon, their status as prostitutes, the power of their professional organ.

The reprise of the beasts' gruntings, answering the grunts of the army mates, sets the women in motion again, their hips, their breasts which, as clouds pass darkly before the moon, they bare to me entirely: If the army mates are talking to animals, they are in high condition to stiffen for women—but without means of payment, how could they penetrate them, touch them even?

On her own—but the pimp, back there, wants money—would one of them at least content herself with the advanced practices of the handsomest—and dumbest—among us, his stolen platinum pocket watch, the ivory-handled knife that his close-retailored fatigues mold to his thigh and with which, rumor has it, he cut off the ears of rebels caught and killed in the caves?

Another one, passing through the gate, long, nearly white hair? It's a barn owl that lands on the post; of the three women, the one who looks the youngest, turned-up nostrils, lowers the top of her body; her breasts sway between the fur of the open raincoat; her fingers spread upon her arched hips; her throat pulses beneath her upraised chin; I swallow back my saliva—on her own, separated from her two shrews—I raise my rifle barrel again; the sound of their ankle boots against the rails has attracted our ensign, a gravestone cutter turned pimp; he descends from the railcar closest to the heavy equipment cars, which, in motion, make a lower, more muted sound than ours; readjusting his belt and fatigues, caressing the underside of his perfumed chin, he descends from the railway bed, approaches the girl: Will he propose to have the handsome one come and satisfy her? The handsomest one of us relieving himself with her, for all the others looking on, in exchange for his platinum watch he stole in a hotel on Place Bresson in Algiers from an international trafficker as a gratuity for a lay? But who would reimburse him the value of the watch? Perhaps he still keeps, in a pocket between his skin and his tightly retailored fatigues, a remainder of the money he received in dollars for the lay? But the platinum watch, if it's real, couldn't it bring in enough for the whole company to go whoring for an entire thirty-six hours' leave?

A little whistled song and here he is, the beauty, cap turned back, lobes shining, lips full, as he hops from the railcar, his fresh hand, beautiful all the way to the fingertips, poised on his heavy packet; no dance on the railway bed as on the parquet of the village ball, his hand sure, unbuttoning himself already at his crotch; the owl takes flight; in the distance, on a back path, white loafers hop onto mud; the beauty puts his other hand into his pocket; knife fight? Our ensign tugs him by the belt toward the railcar; the girls, their hair whitened by the moon's beam, step up onto the platform, toward the black night; the beauty, standing, loins shaking, head cast back upon the void, watch glinting at the delicate joint of his wrist, lets forth a rattle in his own mist... From the far end of the convoy, whistlings: officers summoning the girls back; they walk along the track again, the pimp emerged from the night, following them on the platform path: good money, the right prices, padded benches, toilets, even if deteriorated (but scrubbed, under orders, by a few of us), beers, and in the case of some of the men—subofficers, survivors of Indochina, bodies scarred, Mother Army, minds straying at times over there in the Plain of Reeds—a greater competence in the handling of prostitutes, of which it is said that the ones from over there, affiliated with the Vietcong, would line their small lips with razor blades to mutilate their clientele.

In the afternoon of the following day, the convoy comes to a halt in the Gare de S.; trucks bring us to the camp; we settle into the barracks, bunk beds; odor of leather, coarse linen, grease, creolin; a rumor that we are to be liberated in seven days; tomorrow morning, unload the heavy equipment, reload the trucks, unload in front of the hangars, transport and stock the equipment in the warehouses; three days of muscle, steel, grease, rust, clatter, mud.

One of us, an apprentice pastry chef in Ain, freckled little face, reads, from inside the truck, at a crossroads, on a signpost, the name of a village; it's the name of the village where his father was billeted, a Piedmontese day laborer enlisted very young as a volunteer in 1918, wounded, recalled, and granted citizenship in return for his injury; the downpour blurs the forms, below, above, behind, time, the hours, the years, the decades, the generations: Our little redhead—will he ever be tall enough to slide his pastries into the oven?—His father sways at our side on the slats, in his odor of a young *poilu* ...

The eve of the last day: three of us are assigned to wash a load of cutlery and cookpots from three companies that departed in haste and left their chores unfinished; in the back kitchen, as big as half a hangar, coarse cloth slung over our shoulders, scrapers, brushes in our hands, we soak the dishes in broad vats of hot water: hundreds of plates, glasses, knives and forks, dozens of large cookpots on the inside of which remain crusts of meat that we eat, as a reserve against a time of hunger, before we plunge them into the water; little by little, the cookpots, plates navigate into the vats; our joy at our upcoming deliverance within a night's reach—though for me deliverance remains uncertain, despite some favorable indications received from our fellow soldiers in the offices—makes us forget the goal of our task, and the breaking and playing begins, plates thrown against the walls, glasses crushed, cookpots knocked into each other with ladles; the additional strength we acquired during the unloading, along with the officers' exasperation with a government that has turned the army of conscripts into a force of commonsense resistance against a chain of command of uncertain loyalty and accused of dishonorable conduct—abandonment of many Harkis, belated response to massacres—these preclude any punishment, of which the worst would be to postpone, even for a single day, such a longed-for liberation: on the other side await fiancées, girls all open, lips, heart, organ; employment, work, tools, beasts, machines, bedsheets, feasts, everything there glitters.

The day after a night in which—chess matches with M., then P., then Ph., a puppy belonging to one of us playing with the cockroaches beneath the cots—I repress my anguish, and after a lunch where we exchange addresses (those of our parents, for the most part), NCOs seated at tables under a tent canopy in front of the office of our assembled companies, and assisted by army mates from the conscripted troops, call each of us by name, preceded by our rank or simply "soldier," and hand out the Commemorative Medal for the Maintenance of Order in Algeria, along with our final pay—hardly enough, at the time, to cover five meals at a lunch counter. My turn comes toward the middle; some of my army mates—new ones, from the repatriation journey—having already received their portion, stand at my side, me with medal and service certificate in fist, but still with the same menace at my back, that mass of shoulder-striped uniforms: I would need the whole army to be annulled, and along with it the accusation, the interrogation, the underground prison.

Back in the barracks, we undo our uniforms, slip into our civilian clothes—for life? Military effects handed over to the quartermasters, packs on our backs, we pass the gate, the sentry boxes; at last without rank, we run on cracked asphalt three or four kilometers toward the station, between the sodden beet fields.

Do I have the little chain of my identification tag around my neck or did I return it, with the etched digits of its number? Thousands of us wore it around the neck of their corpse—sometimes with the organs mutilated by which they could have transmitted life, a little of their heart, of their spirit, their breath in the world and the breath of the world in them—laid out in the gorges, on the plateaus, the cobblestones, the sidewalks of Algeria. But with them, gathered to them now, and at this hour still, are all those whose throats were slit, noses, lips, ears mutilated, all those whose eyes were gouged out, limbs dismembered, entrails gutted, all those who fled and were tracked down and slaughtered, all those who were beaten to death, cut to pieces, set on fire, babies dashed against the walls, pregnant mothers ripped open, all those who were raped, tortured, boiled alive, hacked and sawed alive, flayed, driven mad, all those who were humiliated for life, all those who went missing, never found: delayed victims of the original crime of the Conquest.

Toward Paris, toward hunger, toward my father; humiliated, more by myself than by my judges—but determined to do battle; everything is to be reconquered. But with what strength of flesh renewed.

OTHER NEW YORK REVIEW CLASSICS
For a complete list of titles, visit www.nyrb.com.

DANTE ALIGHIERI Paradiso; translated by D. M. Black
CLAUDE ANET Ariane, A Russian Girl
HANNAH ARENDT Rahel Varnhagen: The Life of a Jewish Woman
OĞUZ ATAY Waiting for the Fear
DIANA ATHILL Don't Look at Me Like That
DIANA ATHILL Instead of a Letter
HONORÉ DE BALZAC The Lily in the Valley
POLINA BARSKOVA Living Pictures
ROSALIND BELBEN The Limit
HENRI BOSCO The Child and the River
ANDRÉ BRETON Nadja
DINO BUZZATI The Betwitched Bourgeois: Fifty Stories
DINO BUZZATI A Love Affair
DINO BUZZATI The Singularity
DINO BUZZATI The Stronghold
CRISTINA CAMPO The Unforgivable and Other Writings
CAMILO JOSÉ CELA The Hive
EILEEN CHANG Time Tunnel: Stories and Essays
EILEEN CHANG Written on Water
FRANÇOIS-RENÉ DE CHATEAUBRIAND Memoirs from Beyond the Grave, 1800–1815
AMIT CHAUDHURI Afternoon Raag
AMIT CHAUDHURI Freedom Song
LUCILLE CLIFTON Generations: A Memoir
RACHEL COHEN A Chance Meeting: American Encounters
COLETTE Chéri *and* The End of Chéri
E. E. CUMMINGS The Enormous Room
JÓZEF CZAPSKI Memories of Starobielsk: Essays Between Art and History
ANTONIO DI BENEDETTO The Silentiary
HEIMITO VON DODERER The Strudlhof Steps
PIERRE DRIEU LA ROCHELLE The Fire Within
JEAN ECHENOZ Command Performance
FERIT EDGÜ The Wounded Age *and* Eastern Tales
MICHAEL EDWARDS The Bible and Poetry
ROSS FELD Guston in Time: Remembering Philip Guston
BEPPE FENOGLIO A Private Affair
GUSTAVE FLAUBERT The Letters of Gustave Flaubert
WILLIAM GADDIS The Letters of William Gaddis
BENITO PÉREZ GÁLDOS Miaow
MAVIS GALLANT The Uncollected Stories of Mavis Gallant
NATALIA GINZBURG Family *and* Borghesia
JEAN GIONO The Open Road
VASILY GROSSMAN The People Immortal
MARTIN A. HANSEN The Liar
ELIZABETH HARDWICK The Uncollected Essays of Elizabeth Hardwick
GERT HOFMANN Our Philosopher
HENRY JAMES On Writers and Writing
TOVE JANSSON Sun City
ERNST JÜNGER On the Marble Cliffs
MOLLY KEANE Good Behaviour
WALTER KEMPOWSKI An Ordinary Youth
SIEGFRIED KRACAUER Ginster

PAUL LAFARGUE The Right to Be Lazy
JEAN-PATRICK MANCHETTE The N'Gustro Affair
JEAN-PATRICK MANCHETTE Skeletons in the Closet
THOMAS MANN Reflections of a Nonpolitical Man
LUIS MARTÍN-SANTOS Time of Silence
JOHN McGAHERN The Pornographer
EUGENIO MONTALE Butterfly of Dinard
AUGUSTO MONTERROSO The Rest is Silence
ELSA MORANTE Lies and Sorcery
MANUEL MUJICA LÁINEZ Bomarzo
MAXIM OSIPOV Kilometer 101
PIER PAOLO PASOLINI Boys Alive
PIER PAOLO PASOLINI Theorem
KONSTANTIN PAUSTOVSKY The Story of a Life
DOUGLAS J. PENICK The Oceans of Cruelty: Twenty-Five Tales of a Corpse-Spirit, a Retelling
HENRIK PONTOPPIDAN A Fortunate Man
HENRIK PONTOPPIDAN The White Bear *and* The Rearguard
MARCEL PROUST Swann's Way
ALEXANDER PUSHKIN Peter the Great's African: Experiments in Prose
BARBARA PYM The Sweet Dove Died
RAYMOND QUENEAU The Skin of Dreams
RUMI Gold; translated by Haleh Liza Gafori
RUMI Water; translated by Haleh Liza Gafori
JOAN SALES Winds of the Night
FELIX SALTEN Bambi; or, Life in the Forest
JONATHAN SCHELL The Village of Ben Suc
ANNA SEGHERS The Dead Girls' Class Trip
VICTOR SERGE Last Times
ELIZABETH SEWELL The Orphic Voice
ANTON SHAMMAS Arabesques
ROGER SHATTUCK The Forbidden Experiment: The Story of the Wild Boy of Aveyron
CLAUDE SIMON The Flanders Road
WILLIAM GARDNER SMITH The Stone Face
VLADIMIR SOROKIN Blue Lard
VLADIMIR SOROKIN Red Pyramid: Selected Stories
JEAN STAFFORD Boston Adventure
GEORGE R. STEWART Fire
GEORGE R. STEWART Storm
ADALBERT STIFTER Motley Stones
ITALO SVEVO A Very Old Man
MAGDA SZABÓ The Fawn
ELIZABETH TAYLOR Mrs Palfrey at the Claremont
SUSAN TAUBES Lament for Julia
TEFFI Other Worlds: Peasants, Pilgrims, Spirits, Saints
YŪKO TSUSHIMA Woman Running in the Mountains
LISA TUTTLE My Death
IVAN TURGENEV Fathers and Children
KONSTANTIN VAGINOV Goat Song
PAUL VALÉRY Monsieur Teste
ROBERT WALSER Little Snow Landscape
MARKUS WERNER The Frog in the Throat
VIRGINIA WOOLF Mrs. Dalloway: The First-Edition Text with the Author's Revisions
XI XI Mourning a Breast